CANTERBURY COLLEGE
NEW DOVER ROAD, CANTERBURY
**LEARNING RESOURCES
CENTRE**

Tel: 01227 811166

Please return book on or before date last stamped:

84994

dding

owers

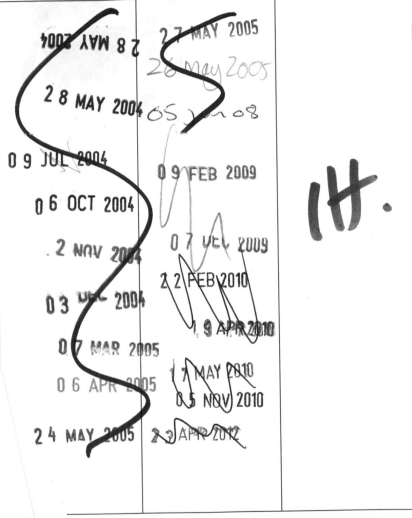

Associate College of the University of Kent

wedding
flowers

Over 80 glorious
floral designs
for that special day

STEPHEN ROBERTS

APPLE

APPLE

First published in the United Kingdom
Apple Press
Sheridan House
4th Floor
112-116A Western Road
Hove
E. Sussex BN3 1DD

www.apple-press.com

This book was conceived and produced by
Breslich & Foss Ltd
2A Union Court
20-22 Union Court
London SW4 6JP

Printed and bound in China

contents

INTRODUCTION

Choosing and planning the flowers for a wedding is an exciting and rewarding task and, for brides who adore flowers, it can be one of the most enjoyable and memorable aspects of the entire event. Whatever the scale and style of the wedding, well-chosen flowers can transform indoor and outdoor locations, making the occasion extra special.

In the following pages, you will find sixteen wedding plans divided into three sections: 'Timeless Classics', 'Seasonal Favourites' and 'Sweet Perfume.' In 'Setting the Scene' (page 10), I look at how inspiration for the wedding flowers can be found in the bride's dress, the season of the year in which the event is to take place, the setting, or the hobbies and interests of the bride and groom.

The core of each wedding plan is the natural beauty of the flowers and foliage used; it is these elements that prevent the 'themes' from becoming too contrived. Each theme takes into account the season, style, setting and scale of the wedding, illustrating how truly beautiful results can be achieved by the use of appropriate floral displays. From the elegance of white moth orchids to the visual impact of red gloriosa, from the restrained simplicity of longiflorum lilies to the jostling abundance of summer garden flowers, you will find these pages bursting with ideas to suit all tastes and budgets.

FLOWERS

Along with designs for bouquets, nosegays, headdresses and boutonnieres, there are plenty of accessible ideas for decorating the reception area. Arches, doorways, canopies, chairbacks, staircases and tables are all given treatments that are fresh, eye-catching and adaptable. One of my aims in this book is to clear away the mystique surrounding how such pieces are made. Many of the designs are easy to construct and can be undertaken by interested brides and their families or friends. However, if you choose one of the grander plans, you may prefer to employ a professional florist or floral decorator.

Wedding Flowers is intended to be inspiring but also very practical, so clear design recipes and construction methods are given for each of the eighty projects. At the end of the book, you will find step-by-step instructions on wiring techniques and other floristry methods. The 'Gallery' provides a visual index to the main items made in the book, and a 'Plant Directory' provides useful information on each of the featured flowers.

I hope that professional florist and bride-to-be alike will find this book to be an invaluable resource of fresh ideas and practical information.

Stephen Roberts

GETTING READY

The three major points to consider when planning your wedding flowers are their importance on the day, your budget and who will undertake the work. Only when you have made decisions about these elements is it sensible to think in detail about exactly which flowers you will have and how their colours will fit into your wedding plan as a whole.

For some brides, flowers are one of the most important aspects of the wedding; for others, they are a minor detail. But no matter how much prominence you feel you would like to give to the flowers, it is important to get the choice and the arrangements right. Flowers can transform a dreary, mundane room, add luscious scent to a marquee and bring out the detail in the bride's and bridesmaids' gowns.

Once you have established how much emphasis you would like to place on the wedding flowers, decide on a realistic budget and stick to it. Unless you have a friend or relation who is knowledgeable about flowers, seek the advice of a professional – especially if the budget is low. A good florist or flower arranger can help you to develop your flower ideas around seasonal choices that will help keep costs down. He or she can also advise you about using flowers with colours that suit your dresses or setting, using the most expensive flowers only at strategic points. But however large or small the budget, the bride should always have the bouquet of her choice, as this is what she will remember for the rest of her life.

Plan ahead

Planning the flowers is the fun part, but as the wedding day approaches, the task of making bouquets, buttonholes, corsages and other arrangements without an army of friends or professional helpers can be extremely daunting. If you or your friends are arranging the flowers, then quantities and types of flower must be determined well in advance of the wedding and orders placed with suppliers. Flowers and greenery donated by friends and cut flowers from the florist should be available at least two days before they are to be used. Once everything has been gathered, the flowers must be prepared and conditioned properly. Unlike flowers for domestic use, which are required to last a long time, wedding flowers must be conditioned so they are open and at the peak of perfection on the big day. Knowing how different flowers respond to various conditioning methods and how to get them into peak condition at the right time is very important. (See 'Care and Conditioning' on page 124 for further information.)

If you decide to get professional help with the flowers, remember that a good florist or floral decorator should be interested in your event and be able to interpret your ideas. The ideal person will guide you into making decisions that will suit your personality, style and the mood you wish to create for the day, while also taking into account the budget. If the person does not ask any questions about the dress or setting, or if he or she keeps asking what you want without making suggestions, then you would do well to look elsewhere. The scale of the wedding is also important. A local florist, however good, may not be experienced in undertaking large-scale floral event work. One way to find out whether a certain florist is suitable is to ask to see photographs of work he or she has done previously.

After booking the florist and choosing the designs, make sure everything is confirmed in writing. You can then forget about the flowers until two or three weeks before the wedding, when you will need to contact the florist to confirm your order and to make any final adjustments. By this time, you should have a more accurate idea of the number of guests to expect and so be able to tell the florist how many tables to decorate, chairbacks to make, and so on. Most florists will place their flower order with suppliers about two weeks before the wedding, so all you have to do on the day is take delivery of the bouquets and buttonholes.

SETTING THE SCENE

Once the initial excitement of the engagement passes, plans usually begin in earnest for the big day. Most brides, bridegrooms and family members planning a wedding have an idealised vision of the day, though they may not realise it. A good way to start is to have a brainstorming session, jotting down anything that comes to mind. Collecting information on all aspects of a wedding helps bring together a whole range of ideas that can then be developed into a workable plan. Consider whether you want an informal, intimate wedding or a grander, more formal day built around a place of worship. If it is to be a secular wedding, would a civil ceremony in an unusual setting be fun? It is answers to questions like these that will allow the day to develop a character of its own and help you make your dream wedding a reality.

Themed weddings

Some couples want their wedding to have a particular look associated with a time period or style. A wedding with a strong theme needs a great deal of planning for it to be successful and not look too contrived. The key to this is control! Certain times of year, such as Christmas, Valentine's Day and Easter, have strong visual images that can be developed for a wedding. Settings can be given a medieval or Elizabethan makeover, for example, and the theme can be carried through the style of the dress, the location and the flowers. In the right setting, a Venetian ball or exotic, Oriental look can work well. The personalities of the bride and groom are crucial when deciding on this sort of theme. Outgoing, extrovert people will enjoy the theatricality of the setting and will rise to the occasion. For brides and grooms with more reserved personalities, however, a subtler theme may be best.

Creating a style board

A style board is a fun way to visualise these initial thoughts and, more importantly, it allows others to see what you have in mind. This approach not only clarifies your ideas, it is also very useful for your florist, as it will help him or her to understand your vision and make it a reality. A number of style boards can be produced for different aspects of the day, but one based on the overall look of the wedding is a good place to start. As we have seen, a place or time of year, a type of flower, or the wish to use a certain colour can all help stimulate initial thoughts and become the starting point for developing and creating an individual look for the wedding.

Style boards should be created at the beginning of the design process, once magazine cuttings, postcards, paint and fabric swatches, flowers and any other inspirational items have been collected. Bear in mind that you may well be putting together a style board in a different season from that of the planned wedding day, so you may have to make use of photographs of your chosen flowers.

BUILDING A FILE

The best way to store tear sheets from magazines and swatches of fabric is in a file: all you need is a good pair of scissors and a loose-leaf binder or scrapbook. If you decide on a loose-leaf binder, use clear plastic sleeves that will protect magazine cuttings, photographs and postcards while allowing you to see them at a glance. Pages in a scrapbook can be headed 'Ceremony', 'Reception', 'Dress' and so on. As images or pictures are found, they can be cut out and stuck in the appropriate section of the scrapbook.

Gather together all the elements you want to put on the style board, placing the most important ones in the centre of the board and arranging the rest in groups around them. To make the board as attractive as possible, try to make sure that each side of the board has a similar amount of darker and paler tones. Play around with the arrangement until you are happy with it, then tape or glue items in place.

From style board to reality

The style board on page 11 was for a bride who loved gardening and spring flowers, but who didn't want everything dominated by bright yellow daffodils. She hoped that the flowers would help give her wedding an elegant, restrained look. By looking through a variety of magazines and cutting out any photographs that she liked for colours, styles and flower types, the bride started to develop a springtime plan. This helped us to establish a style and look that was all her own. The bride's choice of paint swatches, fabric samples and magazine cuttings helped me to develop a plan based on soft cream, lilac and lavender blue. Lavenders and greenish whites were brought in with grape hyacinths and snowdrops, as seen in the bridesmaid's bouquet (overleaf).

Gift boxes decorated with flowers and individual arrangements of campanula wrapped with twigs and moss (left) add to the sense of budding spring in this delicate place setting. The napkins were lightly bound in the same way (above).

The bridesmaid's garland headdress of fine birch twigs and soft lilac campanula and hyacinth pips echoed the spring style, and a delicate straw basket decorated with the same twigs and flowers repeats the country feel.

Soft yellow and lilac combine to make this bridesmaid's bouquet the essence of spring. The heart of the bouquet is strengthened by white parrot tulips.

Seasonal and exotic flowers were blended together in this round open-style bridal bouquet (right) of white moth orchids, stephanotis, hyacinths and campanula. The simplicity of the bouquet ensured that it went well with the rest of the wedding flowers, the lilac-coloured flowers linking it to the place settings and bridesmaids' dresses.

section one...

timeless classics

By taking out the centre of these flamingo flowers, the spathe can be used as a leaf to back a group of perfect ivory Akito roses for a stunning bouquet.

URBAN ELEGANCE
Akito Roses and Flamingo Flowers

The setting for this urban wedding is an interior decorated in off-whites and soft creams with natural wood surfaces. The overall look of the furnishings and fittings is solid and luxurious, while a hint of the country is brought in with spindle-back chairs. Flowers have been chosen to reflect this modern setting. Simple white roses are combined with visually and texturally interesting elements to create unusual arrangements. The bouquet has a limited number of items within it and these are repeated and added to for the rest of the wedding flowers, picking up on the muted tones of the setting.

The bride carries a hand-tied bouquet of Akito roses and flamingo flowers. The white roses are massed together to form the centre of the bouquet and the textured, creamy pink spathes of flamingo flowers are set around the edge. Flamingo flowers are sometimes difficult to use because of the central spadex. However, for this bouquet, the long spadices have been removed by pinching them out at the base.

Bold solid forms make a strong visual statement for this modern nosegay-style bouquet.

A combination of berries and foliage are grouped around a perfect rose for the delicate buttonholes. Mahonia berries, scented pelargonium leaves and echeveria buds are unusual additions that work well to give the traditional rose a modern twist.

An intimate wedding with only a small number of guests is a good opportunity to introduce small floral details that would be difficult on a larger scale. Guests at this wedding are greeted with a glass of champagne beautifully presented on a burnished tray and decorated with a small spray of flowers tied to the stem with ribbon, the floral combination echoing the buttonholes.

The natural wood surface of the breakfast tables is so attractive that it was decided to leave them bare. Plant material in muted tones is chosen, with texture and form playing a key role in the selection. Japanese knotweed is used as the base of the arrangement, though if none grows in your area bamboo makes a good substitute. Sections of stalk are cut, each with a watertight base, and a single white rose is placed in each (see opposite page). King proteas are stripped of most of their sepals and the heads placed directly on the table. Some stalks of Japanese knotweed are left open with the ends cut at an angle, reminiscent of organ pipes,

Champagne glasses decorated with a single rose and some berries make the reception at this small wedding really special.

A white rose surrounded by berries and scented pelargonium leaves makes an unusual buttonhole (above left).

Pillar candles rise out of exotic plant material, creating a strong visual element for this modern wedding.

PLANT MATERIAL

Rosa 'Akito'
Akito rose

Protea cynaroides
King protea

Anthurium andreanum hybrid
Flamingo flower

Fallopia japonica
Japanese knotweed

(or Bambusa
Bamboo)

Pelargonium graveolens
  'Lady Plymouth'
Lady Plymouth pelargonium

Jasminium
Jasmine

Mahonia
Mahonia berries

Flamingo flowers and roses look good against the spindles of the chairs.

and textured ceramic candlesticks with thick, creamy white candles add height to the arrangement. Flamingo flowers and trails of jasmine soften the rigid lines of the centrepiece and echo the chairback decorations. The chairs are decorated with a creamy white Akito rose backed by two flamingo flower spathes, again with the central spadex removed. Two strands of flowering jasmine are wound around the flamingo flowers and rose, softening the overall look.

DESIGN RECIPE

Bouquet:

5 flamingo flowers

9 Akito roses

Buttonhole:

1 Akito rose

2 scented pelargonium leaves

2 sprigs mahonia berry

Each champagne flute:

1 Akito rose

1 scented pelargonium leaf

2 sprigs mahonia berry

Centerpiece:

3 proteas

3 flamingo flowers

4 pieces twisted bamboo

2 full stems Japanese knotweed
    cut into pieces

10 Akito roses

3 pieces jasmine

Foliage to fill

Each chairback:

2 flamingo flowers

1 Akito rose

1 piece jasmine

ASSEMBLY DETAILS

For the **bouquet**, Akito roses are left on natural stems with the leaves and thorns removed. These are support-mounted externally on 22 gauge (0.71 mm) wires. The roses are then arranged in the hand, spiralled around a central rose. Five flamingo flowers have their spadices removed and are arranged at the base of the binding point to form a frame. The bouquet is secured with florist's pot tape and finished with a satin ribbon 25 mm (1 in) wide. An Akito rose has the stem removed and a 22 gauge (0.71 mm) wire inserted into the base of its calyx for the **buttonhole**. This is then taped, and small groups of mahonia berries and echeveria buds are support-mounted on 28 gauge (0.38 mm) silver wires and also taped. Two scented pelargonium leaves are loop-stitched and taped. All the items are grouped around the central rose, with the larger and longer materials at the back and the stems are taped together. The **champagne flutes** are decorated with small floral sprays made in the same way as the buttonhole, except with the addition of a ribbon around the stem of the glass to hold the decorations in place.

The framework for the **centrepiece** is made by laying two pieces of Japanese knotweed stalk parallel to each other, approximately 15 cm (6 in) apart. Two shorter pieces are then laid across these to form a rectangle and secured at the corners with wire (though raffia, string or ribbon could also be used). Groups of stalks are cut into sections, each with a cross-membrane included to keep the 'tubes' watertight. The stalks are filled with water and flowers as required and attached to the frame. Flamingo flowers and jasmine trails are woven through the stalk framework and protea heads are placed around the main structure. For the **chairback decorations**, flamingo flower spathes and a single rose are placed in a test tube, along with a piece of jasmine, and attached to the chair spindles with fine wire.

Flamingo flower spathes, flushed with pink at the edge,s frame a beautiful white Akito rose and look simple but stylish.

COUNTRY HOUSE
Roses and Maidenhair Fern

The grand setting of a large country house is the inspiration for a combination of roses and maidenhair fern. The beautiful open roses and frothy fern are typical of the flowers and foliage that would have been available to a family living in this type of house during its heyday in the eighteenth and nineteenth centuries. Large conservatories, greenhouses and walled gardens would have been filled with a wonderful selection of plants to supply a profusion of colour and scent to grace the main rooms of the house.

An unadorned wedding dress made of beautiful Thai silk needs a bouquet that will not overpower its simple grandeur with masses of mixed plant material, yet the choice of design has to be in keeping with the setting. A special composite-flower arrangement called a Carmen rose, in which extra rose petals are wired around a central open rose, fulfils this requirement perfectly; the effect is of a very large rose full of petals that gives a massed focal point as a counterpoint to the simple dress. Another slightly smaller Carmen rose is set into the bride's hair towards the back and side of her head. Large Osiana roses of a peachy cream colour are used throughout the floral designs. They have a long bud and plenty of petals, making them an ideal flower to use for a Carmen rose bouquet. The groom's buttonhole is made from a single open Osiana rose, repeating the style of the bride's bouquet and headdress.

Brimming with petals, the bride's delicate bouquet is in the grand manner, a style in keeping with the country house setting. Both the Carmen rose bouquet and hair flowers complement the dress with their simplicity.

The bride's bouquet, the groom's buttonhole and flowers for the bridesmaid in delicate tones of ivory and soft blush are ideal for a summer wedding theme.

Flowers of Mexican orange blossom are massed together to form a delicate-looking but sturdy flower ball.

A flower ball is ideal for a very young bridesmaid to carry because its ribbon may be hooked over a wrist or grasped by little fingers quite easily (see above and opposite). This flower ball is made from small groups of Mexican orange blossom flowers and is topped with a small cluster of white rosebuds. A fine, delicate garland of flowers is the most suitable headdress for a young child because it is easily sized to the child's head and comfortable to wear. This garland combines Mexican orange blossom flowers and tiny bud roses.

Classic white table linen allows centrepiece flowers to be seen against a plain, light background and helps them to stand out (see overleaf). Small floral gifts and flower-bedecked chairback ties complete the picture, making a statement without distracting attention from the room itself. A glass-and-gold ormolu bowl is used as the base for the centrepiece. Plant material tumbles out of the bowl and the detail of the gilt legs and garlanding becomes a feature. The shape and form of light green maidenhair fern fronds arched over the container reflect the detail of the gilt decoration. The centrepiece is kept low so that guests can see over the top and continue their conversations unhindered. The low mass of Osiana roses set in a mound of fern fronds, Mexican orange blossom flowers, white shrub roses and delicate umbels of Queen Anne's lace, is reminiscent of the wild plants and flowers growing in the surrounding countryside.

A thick chenille cord and tassel is used as the basis for the chairback ties. A small plastic dish is wired above the tassel and sprays of maidenhair fern arch out from both sides, making a symmetrical framework set against the fabric of the chair covers. Each decoration is completed with two Osiana roses, some Mexican orange blossom flowers and Queen Anne's lace. When viewed together, the table and chairs have a lovely, co-ordinated look that is in keeping with the setting.

TIP When cutting fronds of maidenhair fern, make sure that the leaves are mature. Some immature fronds can wilt a little at the tips. If this happens, cut the tips off; the rest of the frond will be fine.

ASSEMBLY DETAILS

See page 133 for details on how to construct a Carmen rose **bouquet**. The same technique is used for the **headdress**, except that the rose is attached to a hair comb ready to be pushed into the bride's hair rather than into a wet foam holder. For the **buttonhole** a single rose is wired through the base on a 20 gauge (0.90 mm) wire. The wire is cut to length, a piece of Mexican orange blossom is added and both are taped together with florist's green tape.

The **flower ball** is made by wiring sprigs of Mexican orange blossom onto 28 gauge (0.38 mm) mount wires and pushing them into a small, round foam holder that has had its handle removed. Tiny buds of white spray roses are grouped around the top of the flower ball and the cream-and-gold cord handle is attached. For the **bridemaid's headdress,** small groups of Mexican orange blossom flowers and tiny white rosebuds are wired onto 28 gauge (0.38 mm) silver wires. These are then taped to a length of 19 gauge (1.0 mm) florist's headdress wire in layers, alternating Mexican orange blossom flowers and rosebuds, until the required length is reached.

PLANT MATERIAL

Adiantum
Maidenhair fern

Choisya ternata
Mexican orange blossom

Anthriscus sylvestris
Queen Anne's lace

Rosa 'Osiana'
Osiana rose

DESIGN RECIPE

Bouquet:
1 main rose
8 to 10 roses for petals

Headdress:
1 main rose
6 to 8 roses for petals

Buttonhole:
1 rose
1 piece Mexican orange
    blossom

Flower ball:
50 to 60 groups Mexican orange
    blossom flowers
1 stem spray roses

Flower girl's headdress:
12 to 15 groups Mexican orange
    blossom flowers
12 to 15 rosebuds

Centrepiece:
12 roses
2 maidenhair fern plants
6 to 8 pieces Mexican orange
    blossom
6 pieces Queen Anne's lace

Floral gift:
1 rose
4 to 5 pieces maidenhair fern
4 to 5 small leaves for the base
2 to 3 pieces Mexican orange
    blossom
a little Queen Anne's lace

Chairback decorations:
1 maidenhair fern plant
2 roses
2 stems spray roses
2 to 3 pieces Mexican orange
    blossom
3 to 4 pieces Queen Anne's lace

*At the end of the day, keeping
your headdress on straight is tricky
for even the most experienced
bridesmaid!*

JEWEL IN THE CROWN
Cymbidium Orchids and Gloriosa

The richly embroidered ivory silk of this wedding dress gives a regal quality with an Indian influence. The exotic style of the fabric allows for the development of a lovely floral theme with overtones of the Indian subcontinent. The fusion of East with West in the flowers and bride's dress is further enhanced by the eclectic influences found in the reception hall's decor. This style of wedding is suitable for any bride with a sense of adventure!

A bouquet draped across the palm of the hand is easy to hold and looks as different and striking as the dress itself, complementing the fabric and embroidery to create a strong overall look. The base of the bouquet is a silk cord to which a handmade wire mesh has been attached at a number of places. The mesh has an organic flow to it and gives the impression of fine gold filigree, echoing the delicate embroidery of the wedding dress fabric. The light, feathery foliage of asparagus fern contrasts with the exotic shape and rich colour of the gold cymbidium orchids, which form the focal point of the bouquet. Lighter, softer elements are brought in with the red-and-yellow flowers of *Gloriosa superba* 'Rothschildiana'. These are used in a waterfall style, cascading down the cord and golden wire mesh. The wonderful shawl draped over the bride's shoulder is complemented by a long shoulder spray of orchids and gloriosa (see opposite and page 34). The larger flowers are kept to the top of the shoulder spray, helping the visual and actual balance.

Carved wooden screens provide a lovely background for the elegant and exotic wedding dress and flowers.

Table decorations for the reception are simple yet exotic, the feeling of opulence and cultural fusion running through the whole floral design. Linking with the bridal flowers, the centrepiece uses the same golden wire mesh and silk cord construction as its base. The wire mesh and foliage act as an anchoring point for the plastic test tubes hidden in their midst and help keep them in a vertical position so that water does not spill onto the table. The table is decorated further with rose and carnation petals in shades of gold and red, grouped around the base of the central arrangement and also heaped on square gold-coloured plates. Perfumed candles in pretty red-and-gold glasses add the finishing touch to the exotic, opulent look of the whole setting.

The jewel-like colours of the floral shoulder corsage dazzle when set against the gold cord and golden filigree wire mesh.

Golden plates and colorful glass candleholders complement the flowers and petals to make this centrepiece sparkle (right).

Wooden figures greet guests with brightly coloured welcome garlands.

A touch of fun is brought to the reception thanks to a pair of wonderful Indian figures positioned to greet the guests. Each figure carries a brightly coloured garland of carnation heads in shades of pink and gold.

Throughout the reception hall, gourd-shaped vases in a rich golden orange are filled with stems of gloriosa that are used on the vine to soften the outline of the containers (see opposite page, below). An alcove with a curved shelf an ideal place for one of these arrangements.

PLANT MATERIAL

Cymbidium
Cymbidium orchid

Gloriosa superba 'Rothschildiana'
Rothschildiana gloriosa

Asparagus densiflorus 'Myersii'
Asparagus fern

Rosa 'First Red'
First Red rose

Dianthus 'Harvest Moon'
Harvest Moon carnation

Dianthus 'Shocking Pink'
Shocking Pink carnation

ASSEMBLY DETAILS

The free-form gold wire mesh for the **bouquet** and **shoulder corsage** is very easy to make – see the method on page 135. Plant material and beads can be attached to this mesh either by gluing them to the frame or wiring them in place. The **garlands** are made by threading carnation heads onto 24 gauge (0.56 mm) wire. Measure the required length of the garland and cut a piece of wire to the appropriate size. Push the end of the wire through the base of the first flower head and pull it through to leave an end of about 8 cm (3 in). Push the end of the wire through the base of the first flower once more to hold it in place. Continue to thread carnation heads onto the wire until the required length is reached.

TIP To prepare the vases of gloriosa, first tie the stems tied together then place them directly into water that has had flower food added. This will improve the lasting qualities of the flowers. The pollen sacs on gloriosa open quickly. If they are removed as the flower first opens, they will not stain dresses or fingers; if left on, they can stain fabric very easily.

ALTERNATIVES

This type of design demands exotic, vibrant flowers. Bougainvillea or a range of orchids such as *Oncidium* **'Golden Showers' would be suitable. Brightly coloured lilies could also be used.**

DESIGN RECIPE

Bouquet:

Wire mesh: ⅔ reel 24 gauge
(0.56 mm) wire

9 cymbidium orchid heads
5 pieces gloriosa on the vine
3 pieces asparagus fern

Corsage:

Wire mesh: ⅓ reel 24 gauge
(0.56 mm) wire

7 cymbidium orchids
5 gloriosa heads
1 piece asparagus fern

Centrepiece:

9 cymbidium orchids
5 miniature cymbidium orchids
10 stems gloriosa
3 pieces asparagus fern
13 First Red roses
7 carnation heads

Each garland:

25 to 30 carnation heads

Each vase of flowers:

10 stems gloriosa on the vine

Beautiful and exotic, the rich carmine pink petals edged in yellow make gloriosa a striking and unusual flower (above left).

Massed carnation heads layered in clashing colours make a good base for a thick flower garland (above right).

This wonderfully shaped ceramic vase (right) is the perfect container for long stems of gloriosa lilies.

White moth orchids used on
their own are the ultimate
in elegant wedding bouquets .

Bold flower forms echo the curves
and twists of this deep gilt frame
(right), the two complementing
each other beautifully. One of
the whitest of flowers, the moth
orchid adds a touch of brilliance
to the soft grey-green tones
of the foliage.

PUTTING ON THE RITZ
Moth Orchids

This wedding design takes its inspiration from the ornate interior of the reception hall
and the elegant lines of the bride's dress. The overall design of white on white relies
for its success on simplicity of design, strong form and contrast in texture between
flowers and fabric. Orchids are the perfect flower to convey a feeling of opulence; in
combination with the grand reception setting and classic wedding dress, the effect is
one of elegant sophistication.

The bouquet is simple enough not to overwhelm the dress but still has a strength of
form to complement its clean lines. Orchids have a luxurious and exotic look in
keeping with the rich decor of the setting. The moth orchid has a graceful beauty of
colour and form that lends itself to a simple bouquet. Here, the orchids are made
into a slender cascade that echoes the parallel lines of the dress. The classic feel is

PLANT MATERIAL

Phalaenopsis amabilis
Moth orchid

Onopordon
Scotch thistle

Echeveria
Echeveria

Cotoneaster
Cotoneaster

Jasminium
Jasmine

Hedera
Ivy

Liriope
Lily turf

extended to the mantelpiece decoration and corsages for guests. To complement the simplicity of the bride's bouquet, the buttonholes are also centered around a white moth orchid. Three variegated ivy leaves are added to disguise the binding point and two looped lily turf leaves complete the design.

The mixed plant material for a low, wide arrangement set on a lovely gilt console table sets off the ornate frame of the mirror above it (see page 39). Because of the opulent gilt woodwork, the plant material has to be bold and strong in form and shape. Sprays of luxuriant moth orchids form the basis for the arrangement, supported by variegated cotoneaster foliage. Wispy trails of jasmine add a delicate perfume to the display. The arched grey-green downy leaves of the Scotch thistle repeat the shapes in the mirror frame. In the centre of the arrangement, the focal point is a perfect specimen of echeveria. All of the plant material is set in a glass-and-gilt container with scrolled feet. The moth orchid is available in a range of colours, some with attractive and unusual marbling on the petals. However, it is the overall shape, reminiscent of moth wings, that makes the flowers so distinctive.

Set against a dark jacket, the delicate shape of the moth orchid looks at its best.

For the **bouquet,** the orchids are wired individually with 22 gauge (0.71 mm) wires pushed into the base of each flower head. Each flower is then cross-wired with a 28 gauge (0.38 mm) silver wire to prevent it spinning, then taped with white florist's wedding flower tape and mounted on a 15 gauge (2.0 mm) stay wire. Three stay wires of various lengths are taped together with white tape. These are then pushed through a wet foam holder and wired to the cage at the top and bottom to keep the wire from moving. Other flowers (many of these on short natural stems) are pushed into the foam and secured, to form the head of the bouquet. (It is advisable to make this type of bouquet on the morning of the wedding.)

TIP After wiring and before taping, wrap a small, wet piece of cotton wool or tissue around the base of each flower to help keep the orchids fresh and firm.

DESIGN RECIPE

Bouquet:
35 individual orchid flowers

Side table arrangement:
2 moth orchid stems
1 echeveria
5 Scotch thistle leaves
3 cotoneaster sprigs
2 jasmine stems

Centrepiece:
3 moth orchid flowers

Buttonhole:
1 moth orchid
3 ivy leaves
2 lily turf leaves

The simplicity of this centrepiece affords a striking contrasts with the elaborate interior of the hall.

FLOWING LINES
Calla Lilies and Laurel Leaves

The beautiful calla lily lends itself to a variety of floral decoration styles, the elegant shape of the creamy white curled spathe, formed at the top of a long, pale green stem, producing a striking effect. The design for this wedding is centred around the shape of a single calla lily, emphasising the principle that repeating the same form is very effective. This is evident when the flower is used singly as a table decoration or massed on either side of a door as demonstrated on the following pages. Every piece in this wedding scheme allows the shape of the individual flowers to be seen.

This spray of lilies (left) makes a striking door decoration.

Calla lilies make a graceful wedding bouquet (opposite) when stem and flower are used together.

Twisted stems and silver metal rise airily out of a glass bowl (left) and meld together in a free-form arrangement.

A light fitting becomes a major feature when decorated with calla lilies (right).

ALTERNATIVES

Any flowers with a long, flexible stems that will bend easily, such as flamingo flowers or tulips, can be used instead of calla lilies.

Guests are greeted in the entrance hall by a swirl of calla lilies in a large glass bowl set on a circular wood-and-glass table. The glass centre of the table allows light to pass through the whole arrangement, making the flowers look radiant. Metal cone-shaped light fittings are decorated with lilies, the stems curving around the lights to echo the centrepiece design.

A simple spray of calla lilies—with a tight bud at the tip and fully open flowers at the centre—forms a beautiful bouquet, the cascade of flowers complementing the flowing train of the dress (see overleaf). The soft sheen of the satin wedding dress is in harmony with the texture of the lilies and, because of the elegance of the flowers and stems, no foliage is used.

The white arched doorways are framed by simple columns of layered laurel leaves and calla lilies: the backing foliage of dark green laurel helps the individual lilies to stand out, emphasising their shape (see overleaf). The flower heads curve in towards the doorway to enhance both the shape of the flower and the curve at the top of the door. A small spray of laurel leaves and calla lilies is placed in the centre of each door. Door pieces such as these are not only decorative, but can also help guests identify which doors to use within the reception area.

The top table at the wedding breakfast is made of honey-coloured beech. The other tables are arranged around it in a horseshoe shape, with guests sitting along one side of each table. The table decorations are made of calla lilies set in nests of twisted lead-free solder. A small silver ball is pushed into the end of each stem as a decorative feature. These decorations then rest on beds of laurel leaves. The napkins are rolled and secured with a wired laurel leaf to complete the elegant table design.

Sam Edwards

PLANT MATERIAL

Zantedeschia aetheopica
Calla lily

Prunus laurocerasus
English laurel

DESIGN RECIPE

Bouquet:
7 calla lilies

Each door column:
150 English laurel leaves
30 calla lilies

Door spray:
3 calla lilies
5 English laurel leaves

Each table decoration:
1 calla lily
3 Englsh laurel leaves

Glass bowl centrepiece:
8 calla lilies

Each place setting:
1 calla lily

Light fixture decoration:
4 calla lilies

Each napkin:
1 English laurel leaf

*Elegant minimalism is seen in this
restrained wedding table design in
which calla lilies and laurel leaves
are the only floral elements used.*

*At each place setting, a single calla
lily is placed inside an elegant
twist of lead-free solder. These
hold a place card and make an
unusual decoration.*

ASSEMBLY DETAILS

For the **bouquet**, each lily is internally wired, the shorter stems using 22 gauge
(0.71 mm) wire and the longer stems using 20 gauge (0.90 mm) wires. The individual
flowers are layered one on top of the other with the more fully opened flowers at the
heart of the bouquet. The stems are then bound together with green florist's pot tape
before being overbound with white satin ribbon.

Each **door column** is first covered with layered English laurel leaves stapled to a
plywood baseboard 15 cm (6 in) in width. Each calla lily is cut to a height of 30 cm
(12 in), placed in a plastic test tube behind the English laurel leaves and secured to
the baseboard. Low-melt glue gives added support where needed and is hidden by
the layered leaves. The columns can be made a day or two before the wedding as
the lilies are in test tubes filled with water. Each **door spray** is made by loop-
stitching individual laurel leaves with 22 gauge (0.71 mm) wire, taping them then
binding them into a fan shape with florist's corsage tape. Three internally wired calla
lilies, the ends of their stems sealed with glue, are tied to the leaves and the whole
arrangement is attached to the door with florist's pot tape.

The calla lilies used in the **table decorations** have their ends sealed with florist's
glue; this holds in moisture and stops the flowers wilting. (If the flowers are also
sprayed with Oasis Clear Life, then the transpiration rate is further lowered and the
lilies can be used out of water for two to three days.) A silver ball is inserted into
each stem to neaten them.

The flowers in the **glass bowl centrepiece** (see page 44) are glued to a curved wire,
and a nest of twisted, lead-free solder is used as a support.

TIP Make sure calla lilies are well conditioned before they have their ends sealed
with low-melt glue. The glue must cover all of the end and reach about 1 cm (½ in)
up the stem. Always keep lilies in a cool room before they are displayed.

Vases filled with beautiful white cherry blossoms frame the entrance doorway and lead to a light and airy balcony.

Simple sprays of orchids in blue-and-white ginger jars make an exotic centrepiece (right).

ORIENTAL SPRING
Vanda Orchids

This stylish wedding has a strong Oriental influence based on the creamy beige cheongsam chosen by the bride. When the embossed silk of the dress catches the light, subtle lilac and mauve tones appear within the fabric. The clean lines of the cheongsam are reflected in the elegant simplicity of the wedding flowers.

Vanda orchids are chosen for the bouquet because their colour and shape complement the style and fabric of the dress. The rich, clear mauve of the orchid with its marbling in lighter mauve running across each petal, makes this flower one of nature's most striking creations. Because the colour of the vanda orchid is so strong and the style of the cheongsam is so simple, a plain, unfussy bouquet works best. Two stems of vanda orchids, each with six or seven perfect flowers, are used without foliage so that nothing detracts from the beauty of the flowers. Because simplicity is a key factor in the style of the wedding flowers, the bride wears a single vanda

*Stems of vanda orchids make a
suitably exotic bouquet. The
simple headdress has spiked drops
of white hyacinth flowers
suspended from cornus stems.*

orchid in her hair secured by two spikes of dogwood, the ends of which are finished off with 'tassels' of hyacinth pips that have been threaded together.

Traditional blue-and-white Chinese pottery is the anchor point for the rest of the wedding-flower theme. The delicate pattern of cherry blossoms within the fabric of the cheongsam is repeated in the branches of blossom placed in large blue-and-white Chinese vases throughout the reception hall and also leading onto a pretty balcony. White cherry blossom placed on either side of the head table frame the couple, and the profusion of blossom mirrors the blossom motif on each vase and adds a feeling of abundance to the overall look.

The Chinese influence is continued throughout the rest of the room with a selection of blue-and-white ginger jars filled with vivid mauve vanda orchids. Carved wooden stands raise the jars off the tables, showing the flowers to their best advantage. A single head of vanda orchid is laid at each guest's place setting, filling the table with colour.

ASSEMBLY DETAILS

For the **bouquet**, each orchid stem is carefully supported by 20 gauge (0.90 mm) wire twisted down the stem in between the individual flowers. This support means the stems look delicate but will stand up to the events of the day. The two stems are also lightly bound with ribbon where they are to be held by the bride. This type of orchid lasts well out of water; however, if the day is expected to be very hot, the ends of the stems can be placed in a little vial of water plugged with a rubber cap to prevent leaking. The vial could either be covered with tape to match the flower stem or bound with a delicate ribbon.

For the **vases of cherry blossom**, cut stems that have flowers in bud or that will open the day before you want to use them. Early morning is the best time, as this is when the transpiration level is at its lowest. Once cut, place the stems in a deep bucket of tepid water containing flower food for shrubs or woody-stemmed plant material and allow them to condition for at least six hours before using them.

section two...

seasonal favourites

Grasses, seed heads and berries
are an unusual combination of
seasonal plant material.

Textured simplicity and restraint in plant
selection is the key to success in this crescent
headdress (above right).

SEASON OF MELLOW FRUITFULNESS
Berries and Autumn Flowers

Seasonality is always an important factor to take into account when selecting the flowers for a wedding. Choosing plant material that reminds us of a time of year lends a sense of place and time to an occasion. This is never more evident than in the autumn with the wonderful array of grasses, seed heads, berries and fruits that bring interest in form, shape, texture and colour.

The colour and texture of the wedding dress always helps to determine the plant material; in this case, plants have been chosen to reflect the lovely red velvet bodice and enhance the overall autumnal look. A light open bouquet allows the dramatic dress to be glimpsed through the flowers (see overleaf). A mass of viburnum tinus berries set deep in the bouquet is surrounded by an open framework of stripped and intertwined honeysuckle stems, their colour exactly matching the velvet of the bodice. Bi-coloured roses with a rich red centre and creamy petal undersides coupled with soft gold Peruvian lilies are kept close to the centre of the bouquet, allowing the fine

tracery of burgundy-toned grasses and honeysuckle stems to be seen. To complement the dress and bouquet, the headdress continues the autumn theme. By using only one plant form – berries – the headdress has a texture and shape with a strong character. Worn without a veil, the delicate St John's wort berries look pretty against the stylish, mid-length cut of the bride's hair. The availability of these berries throughout most of the year means that a bride may choose this to have this type of headdress in the winter and late summer months, too.

The reception room with rich, patterned wallpaper influences the overall look of the wedding flowers: a room with such strong character cannot be ignored when it comes to planning the flowers. The bouquet picks up the rich colour tones of the background. These tones are carried through into the flower selection and style of the other floral arrangements, which are soft and flowing with a feeling of abundance in keeping with the season.

The arrangement that tumbles over the edge of the mantelpiece is composed of a combination of plant material. The protea adds an exotic twist to the roses, lilies and berries, its coral colour and sea anemone form providing a contrast with the more solid shapes of the roses and lilies.

Seedpods from Spanish broom and trails of honeysuckle are clearly defined against the white mantelpiece. The Peruvian lily 'Butterscotch', with its soft golden tones and accents of burgundy, adds further richness to the display.

Rich red tones and deep golds look wonderful set against the deep red and cream of the wedding dress.

Texture, form and colour all play their part in the mantelpiece design.

The abundant, flowing style of the mantelpiece arrangement is carried through to the centrepiece. Here again, the use of berries adds a richness that is reflected in the patina of the furniture within the rooms. Beautiful white lace tablecloths and damask napkins contrast nicely with the autumn colours and provide a crisp background for the arrangements. Strands of Spanish broom wrap the napkins and, together with a single bi-coloured Vicky Brown rose, make unusual decorations.

A mass of different flowers can overpower a simple cake, but here (left) autumn berries act as a wonderful contrast to the pristine white icing. To allow the cake to be seen, just the base of each tier is wreathed in a garland of St John's wort berries. To complete the look, a small cluster of berries is placed on the top of the cake, providing a seasonal alternative to sugar flowers or elaborate icing.

Simple circles of berries enhance the classic design of the wedding cake.

Guests are enticed to the table by the combination of berries and flowers used in both the centrepiece and the napkin ties.

Not one to miss a good meal, the family pet is definitely looking her best in this floral collar.

The simple dog collar may be taken off quickly if the dog becomes unhappy wearing it. However, this dog seemed to forget she was wearing anything out of the ordinary! Plant material is selected that won't be harmful if eaten and the collar is constructed so that it is comfortable and safe for the dog to wear.

ALTERNATIVES

A wide range of rosehips in numerous shapes and colours, as well as rowan berries, are available in the late summer and early autumn. Northern red oak has lovely yellow to red-brown leaves in the autumn.

PLANT MATERIAL

Hypericum
St John's wort

Viburnum tinus
Viburnum tinus

Spartium junceum
Spanish broom

Lunaria
Honesty

Grass seed heads

Lonicera
Honeysuckle

Rosa 'Vicky Brown'
Vicky Brown rose

Protea
Protea

Lilium 'Vienna Blood'
Vienna Blood Lily

Alstroemeria 'Butterscotch'
Butterscotch Peruvian lily

ASSEMBLY DETAILS

The basis of the **bouquet** is a wet foam bouquet holder. The intertwined frame is created by using pieces of honeysuckle stripped of leaves, which are then pushed into the holder like the spokes of a wheel. These are then twisted through each other in the same direction and caught with fine, 30 gauge (0.32 mm) silver stub wires. This keeps the outer twisted frame away from the holder and gives a lightness to the bouquet. The base is then covered with bunches of viburnum berries pushed into the foam. Roses, Peruvian lilies, grasses and St John's wort berries are added to complete the design. For the **headdress**, individual St John's wort berries and small groups of berries are wired onto 28 gauge (0.38 mm) silver stub wires and taped with green florist's tape. A 22 gauge (0.71 mm) stay wire is covered with tape, then the taped-and-wired berries are themselves taped onto the stay wire in a layered fashion. The groups are widened towards the centre to create the required crescent shape. This is repeated and the two halves are joined together. The entire headdress is secured to a hair comb with a fine shoelace satin ribbon. The **dog collar** and **cake decorations** are made in the same way as the headdress, except that the separate wired berries are layered and taped onto a 20 gauge (0.90 mm) stay wire. The ends are brought together and taped to complete the cake garland; the two ends of the dog collar are bent over and loosely hooked into one another.

Both the **mantelpiece** display and **centrepiece** are constructed on blocks of floral foam anchored by florist's pot tape to shallow black plastic dishes deep enough to hold about 5 cm (2 in) of water. The foam should be slightly higher than the sides of the containers so that the plant material can flow over the edge. Plant material is simply inserted into the dampened foam. The **napkin rings** are made by forming two or three strands of Spanish broom into a loose circle and securing the ends with a 28 gauge (0.38 mm) florist's silver wire. The rose has a 22 gauge (0.71 mm) green stub wire inserted into its base so it can be faced upwards. It is then bound with corsage tape and secured to the Spanish broom ring at the binding point.

DESIGN RECIPE

Bouquet:

10 pieces honeysuckle

10 to 15 pieces grass

1 honesty stem

10 viburnum stems with berries

5 Vicky Brown roses

2 Peruvian lily stems

4 to 5 St John's wort stems

Headdress:

3 St. John's wort stems

Dog collar:

3 St John's wort stems

Cake decoration:

15 St John's wort stems

Mantelpiece:

6 to 9 Vicky Brown roses

6 to 8 Vienna Blood lily stems

4 protea heads

3 to 4 Peruvian lily stems

5 St John's wort stems

3 Spanish broom stems

Mixed seasonal foliage

Centrepiece:

10 to 12 Vicky Brown roses

9 to 10 Vienna Blood lily stems

4 protea heads

5 to 6 Peruvian lily stems

8 St John's wort stems

4 Spanish broom stems

Mixed seasonal foliage

Napkin ring:

1 Vicky Brown rose

Small part of a Spanish

broom stem

TIP Use berries and fruits that are underripe so that their juices will not stain fabrics.

TULIP SPLENDOUR
Parrot Tulips

Spring is a beautiful time of year for flowers because of the vast range of bulbs available. Tulips in particular are found in many shapes and colours and blend well with different types of fabric and styles of dress. Because they are reasonably priced, they can be used in great profusion without exceeding a modest flower budget. Here, massed parrot tulips and classic tulips in a lovely mid-pink are closely blended to create a dramatic effect.

Hand-tied posies are effective and simple, and tulips are one of the best flowers to use for this style of bouquet. Parrot tulips come in a wide range of colours and here the variety 'Weber' is used to great effect. Each individual flower head is a soft cream with many of the petals flecked with green and pink, their ragged edges giving the bouquet a lacy appearance. A bow of rich cream ribbon finishes the bouquet and the same ribbon is used to bind and cover the stems.

The handsome marble fireplace is a major feature in the reception room and, by enhancing it with flowers, it becomes a focal point for the celebration. Square glass tanks of varying heights and sizes are arranged in small groups, each tank filled with either Weber parrot tulips or mid-pink Christmas Dream tulips, the colours blending together across the mantelpiece (see pages 66–7). The arrangement is further enhanced with small glass tanks filled with tulip petals and topped with perfumed candles. Glass tanks are relatively inexpensive to buy and, when massed together, create a visually effective large design.

The carving on this classic marble mantelpiece are reflected in the shapes formed by the massed flower heads.

Guests sit at long tables that have tanks of tulips arranged down the centre (see overleaf). Individual arrangements decorate at each place setting. A collar of box foliage edges each tank, enhancing the compact, chunky feel of the floral display.

It is often difficult to create large-scale designs using tulips, but here this is overcome by decorating the reception area with willow and tulip 'trees' that are 1.8 metres (2 yards) tall. Stems and branches of red osier dogwood and blueberry are added to the top of the willow arrangement above the moss collar. Plastic test tubes hidden within the trees and filled with parrot tulips create a wonderful blossom effect.

Tulip trees made from groupings of willow stems are used as freestanding decorations in the dining room.

Tanks packed with tulips of one colour are grouped together to form a simple yet unusual mantelpiece design.

ASSEMBLY DETAILS

For the **bouquet,** tulips are first cut to a length of 25 cm (10 in). The tulips for the outer edge of the bouquet are support-wired with 22 gauge (0.71 mm) green plastic-coated stub wires. The first, central tulip is held about halfway down the stem. The others are spiraled around this point to form a nosegay-style bouquet; the wired tulips used at the outer edge help support and protect the other flowers. The bouquet is then taped at the binding point to secure the stems and the group of stems is covered with ribbon 5 cm (2 in) wide. The ribbon is tied in a bow to finish the bouquet.

The box collars around the **glass tanks** are made by bending four square pieces of wire mesh to hook over each side of the container. The mesh is then bent up and away from the container to make a shelf. Pieces of soaked wet oasis are taped to the mesh and the pieces of box inserted into them. Tulips are then cut to length and massed in the tank. Finally, the tank is filled with flower food solution to prolong the life of the tulips. For the **tulip tree,** two willow poles are placed approximately 40 cm (16 in) apart in an upright position. Keeping the bottom of each pole in the same position, the poles are angled so that they cross just above the centre. A third pole is added to create a tripod and the three poles are taped together at the point at which they cross. The rest of the poles are added in a similar way to strengthen the structure. The red osier dogwood and blueberry stems are added by pushing the stems into the binding point from the top to form a tracery of branches. Plastic test tubes filled with water and covered with green tape are wired into position in the upper branches. Each one has a tulip stem placed in it to form a mass of flowers similar to the blossoms on a tree. Finally, Spanish moss is tucked into the willow poles at the binding point to conceal the tape used to hold the poles in place.

TIP To guarantee a particular colour and type of tulip, buy Dutch tulips. These tulips are forced to flower as early as December. However, the greatest range of colours and types tend to be available between January and May. Stems of tulips can still grow up to 48 hours after being cut and arranged, so check the stem lengths just before displaying them and trim as necessary.

PLANT MATERIAL

Tulipa Parrot group 'Weber'
Weber parrot tulip

Tulipa 'Christmas Dream'
Christmas Dream tulip

Buxus sempervirens
Box

Salix
Willow

Cornus sericea 'Flaviramea'
Dogwood

Vaccinium corymbooum
Highbush blueberry

Tillandsia usneoides
Spanish moss

DESIGN RECIPE

Bouquet:
15 Weber parrot tulips

Mantel and centrepieces:
Each small glass tank:
20 tips box foliage
4 to 6 tulip heads

Each large glass tank:
40 to 50 tips box foliage
6 to 9 tulip heads

Tulip tree:
15 willow poles
2 bundles red osier dogwood
2 bunches blueberry
30 parrot tulips
Spanish moss

Glass candleholder:
petals from 2 tulips

ALTERNATIVES
Use hyacinths daffodils, or any other spring flower that has a solid, round head.

A wealth of primroses and white violets massed together greet guests at this spring wedding (left).

The same flowers are featured in the bride's bag – a pretty alternative to the traditional bouquet.

SPRING ABUNDANCE
Primroses

The essence of spring is captured in the profusion of primroses and violets that welcome guests to this wedding. Choosing the right decorations for the setting is crucial for a successful floral plan and the fragile primrose and violet blooms are the choice perfect to decorate the delicate wrought iron spiral staircase in the reception hall of this country hotel.

The pretty wedding dress echoes the simple beauty that is paramount to the success of the wedding theme and a satin bride's bag brimming with primroses and violets adds to the look of spring abundance. The staircase is massed with primroses in mossed pots, grouped on each tread of the stairs. The banister rail is kept free so that guests may still use the stairs easily. The effusion of soft yellow primroses and pale pink violets is a charming and unusual way of decorating this staircase, and the plants are grouped in such a way as to create a drift of colour that moves in turn from pale pink and the palest of lemon yellow to some slightly richer tones.

ALTERNATIVES
A whole range of pot-grown plants such as bellflowers, African violets and Cape primroses would be suitable alternatives, as would a number of flowering alpines such as mossy saxifrage.

The moss-covered pots are allowed to be seen and create the effect of a bloom-studded mossy bank framing the staircase. The white violets add a bright, clean tone that counterbalances the deep green of the moss and prevents it becoming too dominant. The curved window half way up the staircase is also massed with primroses and violets, spring branches just breaking into bud adding a further element of spring exuberance.

Simple willow cones filled with primroses and white violets (see opposite) enable the floral theme to be brought into the church and the reception room. The visual weight of the large primrose plants is kept to the top and bottom of the design while lighter white violets add interest to the middle. Primroses and violets are set in a mossed bowl wrapped with delicate twigs for centrepiece arrangements. The centre of the main bowl holds a glass chimney with a candle in it that can be lit in the early evening to add a warm glow to the guest tables. A book is provided so that guests can write personal messages that the bride and groom will treasure.

ASSEMBLY DETAILS

For the **staircase arrangement**, young plants with plenty of flowers, some open and some in bud, are used. The plants are soaked in a bucket of shallow water a few days before the wedding to moisten the roots, with great care taken not to let the plants sink into the water, as the flowers and foliage must be kept clean. The primroses are left in their plastic pots with a wire pushed through the rim of the pot to use as a plant hanger. The violets are wrapped in black plastic cut into strips big enough to make a watertight package of soil and root to allow the plant to live. Each of the plants is wrapped in moss and attached to a staircase baluster with fine wire.

For the **wicker cones** and the **bride's bag**, the plants are taken out of their pots and the root balls wrapped in black plastic. The cones and satin bag are carefully lined with clear plastic to prevent damage and plants are inserted with moss added to cover any black plastic that may be showing.

PLANT MATERIAL

Sphagnum
Sphagnum moss

Primula vulgaris Wanda Group
Primroses

Violet
Violet

Salix contorta
Twisted willow

Spiraea 'Arguta'
Arguta spirea

Betula
Birch

DESIGN RECIPE

Each 91 cm (yard) staircase decoration:

12 pale pink primrose plants
12 yellow primrose plants
18 bedding-plant-sized white violet plants
1 medium bag moss

Each wicker cone:

3 yellow primrose plants
1 pink primrose plant
2 white violet plants
1 handful moss

Bride's bag:

2 primrose plants
1 white violet plant
4 spirea stems

Window sill:

4 pink primrose plants
4 yellow primrose plants
10 white violet plants
6 twisted willow stems
8 handfuls moss

Each centrepiece:

3 pink primrose plants
3 yellow primrose plants
8 white violet plants
3 handfuls moss
2 birch branch stems

Violets tumble out of a moss-and-twig ring to create a delightful centrepiece (opposite).

Primulas and violets in wicker cones can enliven any indoor or outdoor setting.

THE ETERNAL CIRCLE
African Violets and Lichen

The eternal circle is used as a symbol throughout this winter wedding, epitomised by the bride's wreath of hyacinths, African violets, Lenten roses and lichen. Flowers in rich colours are chosen as they look vibrant even in a poor winter light. A seasonal element is brought in with the liberal use of beautifully textured lichen moss in subtle silver and grey tones, and hyacinths contribute both colour and a delightful scent.

The rich hues of hyacinths, Lenten roses and African violets add a strong colour harmony of violet blues to pinkish reds. The bride carries a floral wreath as a symbol of eternal love and the co-ordinating headdress is a crescent shape. The lichen in delicate silver and grey-green tones adds wonderful texture to both designs.

A tiny corsage is made to nestle in the fur trim of the bride's coat (see overleaf). At the centre of the corsage is a beautiful Lenten rose. The colour of young Lenten roses is fairly strong; but as the flowers age, they take on more subtle, muted tones, often overlaid with hints of green. Purple hyacinths and an African violet flower in jewel-like cerise bring richer tones to the corsage.

A wreath symbolising the eternal circle is a wonderful and unusual bouquet for this winter wedding.

Massed flowers are combined to create this beautiful crescent headdress (below), designed to be worn without a veil.

Sharing elements with the bride's wreath and headdress, the men's buttonhole is a little different yet in keeping with the rest of the wedding flowers.

To complement the bride's flowers, buttonholes for the men combine a seasonal mix of twigs and flowers. Interesting materials are used and the design is kept small and in keeping with the occasion. Larch twigs covered with lichen are the basis for the design and, instead of using one main bloom in the centre, flowers are grouped around the lichen twigs. The contrasting textures of the velvety African violet and the silky satin hyacinth work well together, the whole combination standing out against the dark colour of the men's suits.

The symbol of the circle is found at the reception in the form of chairback wreaths in two different designs (see overleaf). Both designs are based on rings of natural lichen, the colour of the pale green leather chair seats. Lichen wreaths in pale grey-green are tied onto each chair with a lilac ribbon and the colour contrast is most effective. Around each table, alternating chairback wreaths have Lenten roses and African violets added to the basic lichen ring.

A miniature corsage attached to the bride's coat gives a burst of colour to the lovely fur trim.

PLANT MATERIAL

Hyacinthus orientalis
Hyacinth

Helleborus orientalis
Lenten rose

Saintpaulia
African violet

Larix
Larch

Lichen
Lichen

Dianthus
Carnation

All kinds of desserts can be made to look more attractive with the addition of flowers. Here, a luscious berry-filled meringue heart brings an extra element of fun to the occasion, the berries and grapes creating a wonderful contrast against the creamy white of the meringue. Displayed on a bed of flower heads in vivid colours and encircled with a floral wreath at the base of the cake stand, this dessert makes an attractive end to the wedding meal.

The natural texture and colour of this lichen chairback decoration perfectly complements the natural wood furniture. The alternative, flower-strewn wreath is seen on the chair behind.

Set in a smart, modern restaurant, this stylish wedding reception ends with a dessert of meringue and berries set on a glass cake stand decorated with flowers.

DESIGN RECIPE

Bride's wreath:

12 to 15 pieces lichen

9 or 10 Lenten roses

1 blue hyacinth

1 pink hyacinth

1 plant pink African violets

1 plant purple African violets

Bride's corsage:

1 Lenten rose

3 blue hyacinth flowers

3 pink hyacinth flowers

3 pieces lichen

Headdress:

½ raceme blue hyacinth

½ raceme pink hyacinth

½ plant blue African violet

½ plant burgundy African violet

1 Lenten rose

8 small pieces lichen

Each buttonhole:

5 pink hyacinth flowers

2 blue hyacinth flowers

2 pieces lichen-covered larch
  twig

Each chairback decoration:

30 pieces lichen
  (plus a selection of flowers for
  the alternative wreaths)

Dessert decoration:

Around the meringue:

4 racemes blue hyacinth

3 carnations

*Around the base of
the cake stand:*

10 Lenten roses

1 plant blue African violet

1 plant burgundy African violet

1 raceme pink hyacinth

1 raceme blue hyacinth

20 to 25 pieces lichen

ASSEMBLY DETAILS

For the **bride's wreath,** lichen is glued onto a metal wreath ring 30 cm (12 in) in diameter until it is covered. Flower heads are wired onto 28 gauge (0.38 mm) silver wires and taped with green florist's tape. The flowers are then grouped together to make small clusters and wired onto the metal frame in front of the lichen. Extra pieces of lichen and hyacinth flowers are glued to the frame, using a warm-melt glue, to create a flowing pattern. The **chairback decorations** are made in the same way except that a smaller, 25 cm (10 in) metal wreath ring is used. Alternate lichen only and lichen and flower wreaths and attach them to the chairs with lilac ribbon 5 cm (2 in) wide.

The **bride's corsage** is made by wiring the central Lenten rose on 24 gauge (0.56 mm) wire and taping it with florist's tape. All other items are wired on 28 gauge (0.38 mm) silver wire and taped. Each piece is added around the central flower, some tucked in under the binding point and others extended by about 1 cm (½ in) to add interest to the design. The **headdress** is based on a taped, 20 gauge (0.90 mm) stay wire about 15 cm (6 in) in length. Each individual item of plant material is wired onto a 28 gauge (0.38 mm) silver stub wire and taped. Starting from one end, items are added and taped into place in a layered fashion making a rope 2.5 to 5 cm (1 to 2 in) in width. The crescent-shaped headdress is finished by cutting away the excess wire and attaching it to a hair comb with fine shoelace satin ribbon.

The **buttonhole** design is based on two pieces of lichen-covered twig. A closed hook is made at the end of a 28 gauge (0.38 mm) silver stub wire and the pink hyacinth flowers are threaded on one at a time. The end flower is then taped to hold them all in place. Other plant material is wired on a 28 gauge (0.38 mm) wire and taped. The individual items are grouped around the lichen on the central twig and taped at the binding point, letting the bare twig become the stem and remain visible. For the **dessert decoration,** carnation petals are sprinkled onto the glass plate and single blue hyacinth flowers are arranged in a tightly packed fashion around the dish on top of the petals. Two small Lenten roses are added to the edge of the meringue itself. The decorative ring around the base of the glass dish is made in the same way as the bride's wreath.

TIP African violets will last well out of water and work well when glued or wired into a design.

ALTERNATIVES
**Violets, small rosebuds and
moss would work well for
this type of floral theme.**

GRAND ROMANCE

Rhododendrons, Magnolias and Camellias

All through spring, the flowering shrub world comes into its own, especially with the wonderful colours and flower types of rhododendrons, magnolias and camellias. These blooms are truly exquisite, ranging from the palest tones and most delicate flowers to the wonderfully big, blowsy rhododendron heads in a myriad of vibrant shades. Many of these blooms may look fragile, but this underplays their lasting qualities and hardy nature. The shadings and subtle combinations of colours make them ideal as bouquet flowers when set against delicate fabrics such as satin and organza. The arrangements for this spring wedding are grand in style, and use shades of soft cream and pink with touches of rich cerise and carmine red.

The simple buttonhole (above) uses an exquisite bloom as its main component set against glossy foliage and individual lily petals.

This bouquet is in the softest and most delicate shades of pink.

Perfect flower heads nestle among
lush foliage in a celebration of all
that is beautiful in spring flowers
(right).

Spring shrubs and flowers transform
an oak staircase (far right) into an
imposing and grand entrance.

Staircases can be turned into grand entrances down which the bride can descend to the wedding ceremony and guests can reach the reception room. For this wedding, guests are received in a large entrance hall and ushered to a second-floor reception room by way of a beautiful oak staircase wreathed in a garland of mixed flowering shrubs and bulbs. The soft creams and pale pinks of the rhododendrons and camellias are in harmony with the mellow tones of the wood. The colour scheme is kept deliberately soft, with hints of deeper tones brought in for occasional emphasis. As a finishing touch, massed rhododendron flowers are grouped in a shallow container and placed on top of the newel post at the bottom of the staircase.

A weathered stone urn filled with a profusion of spring shrubs is placed in a recess at the top of the staircase and sets the tone for the wedding reception flowers (see overleaf). No rigid pattern is used here and the flowers are allowed to be natural and free, with lilies and apple blossom joining the celebration of a spring country garden. The setting for this type of arrangement is very important and the classic arched recess makes a perfect frame for the design.

The grand yet natural style of arranging used throughout the wedding flowers is used to great effect in the centrepiece. A flat stone urn with a square pedestal foot lifts a medley of blooms above the table. Pale blush rhododendrons are massed together, while buds of magnolia burst out of the top of the arrangement. Camellia and rhododendron foliage is added to frame some of the blooms, enhancing their beauty. To counter the grand style of the centrepiece, napkins are decorated simply with a single Corsican hellebore flower.

The bride's bouquet relies on top-quality flowers for its impact. Camellias in soft pink and white with delicate blush-coloured rhododendrons are combined with sprigs of cherry blossom to form the main part of the bouquet. Camellia leaves are placed carefully to define the individual flowers, acting as a contrast to the pretty blooms and giving the bouquet added structure. A little piece of cherry blossom links the buttonhole (see page 80) to the bride's bouquet. Based on an exquisite white camellia, this unusual buttonhole design uses individually wired lily petals to create a *fleur-de-lys* effect, backed with dark, glossy camellia leaves.

A classic weathered stone urn makes a marvellous container for this arrangement of flowering spring shrubs and flower.

ASSEMBLY DETAILS

The **bouquet** is based on a plastic wet foam holder that has first been soaked for ten minutes in flower food solution. The foliage is cut to length and the stem ends inserted into the foam, with any delicate or edge pieces given extra support by wiring them onto the plastic cage. The cherry blossom is added next, followed by flower heads of camellia and individual rhododendron flowers that have been support-wired with 24 gauge (0.56 mm) stub wire, cross-plied with a 28 gauge (0.38 mm) silver stub wire, then taped. Other leaves are added at the back of the holder to cover up any plastic or foam. For the **buttonhole**, individual leaves and petals are loop-stitched with fine 28 gauge (0.38 mm) silver stub wire then bound with green florist's tape. The main flower is wired on two 28 gauge (0.38 mm) silver stub wires, cross-plied to add strength, then taped. The leaves are grouped at the back and the main flower is added to the centre. Other materials are added as necessary. The wired stems are then pulled together, cut to length and taped.

Garlands can be constructed in many ways, but for the staircase a specially made plastic garland cage is used. The plastic cages are filled with wet foam soaked in flower food solution and the base foliage is cut to length and pushed into the foam. This produces a framework and allows the total width of the garland to be gauged. Flowers are added in groups or individually, going about half way around the garland, which is then attached to the staircase with lengths of ribbon. Final adjustments are made to the flower positions once the garland is in place. The garlands can be made in a workroom, placed in a cardboard box and taken to the wedding hall; if the temperature of the building is cool, they can be fixed in position the day before the wedding.

To make the arrangement in the large **stone urn**, a large plastic bowl is chosen to fit the urn and two plastic frogs are anchored to the bottom of it with oasis fix. A piece of plastic foam is added to reach about 5 cm (2 in) above the edge of the bowl. (By not filling the bowl completely with foam, a good reservoir of water is ensured.) The entire top of the bowl is then covered with wire mesh to support the heavy, woody stems to be used in the design. The framework of the arrangement is made with the heaviest stems, then finer, lighter material is added to the outer edge. Finally the main flowers are pushed into place. The **centrepiece** for the dinner table is made in exactly the same way but on a smaller scale and with more emphasis on plant material flowing over the sides.

TIP Condition spring shrubs and young foliage well before using them and always arrange in water or wet foam to which flower food has been added.

PLANT MATERIAL

Rhododendron
Rhododendron

Camellia japonica
Camellia

Magnolia x *soulangeana*
Magnolia

Lilium
Lily

Helleborus corsicus
Corsican hellebore

Acer platanoides
Norway maple

Tulipa 'Weber'
Weber parrot tulip

Zantedeschia aethiopica
 'Green Goddess'
Green Goddess calla lily

Prunus
Cherry blossom

Malus
Apple blossom

Hedera
Ivy

Perfect camellia flowers and magnolia buds look dramatic against deep green foliage.

DESIGN RECIPE

Bouquet:

10 camellia flowers

5 rhododendron flowers

10 pieces cherry blossom

Camellia foliage

Each buttonhole:

1 piece camellia, including
  3 leaves

1 lily head

1 piece cherry blossom

Each yard (91 cm) garland:

3 rhododendron racemes

4 pieces magnolia

10 pieces camellia

5 tulips

7 pieces Norway maple

Ivy, camellia and
  rhododendron foliage to fill

Floral urn:

5 pale rhododendron racemes

3 pieces magnolia

7 pieces camellia

5 stems pale pink lily

5 stems cerise lily

5 long pieces apple blossom

5 calla lilies

3 pieces Corsican hellebore

5 branches Norway maple

Foliage to fill

Centrepiece:

2 rhododendron racemes

2 magnolia stems

7 pieces pale camellia

5 pieces deep pink camellia

3 pieces Corsican hellebore

Camellia and rhododendron
  foliage to fill

ALTERNATIVES

**Hydrangeas, sweet peas,
delphiniums and lilies would
all be very effective in this
style of arrangement.**

section three...

sweet perfume

ECHOES OF ART DECO
Longiflorum Lilies and Maidenhair Fern

Longiflorum lilies with their trumpet-shaped flowers and long, slender stems are the epitome of elegance and grace. These lilies, along with maidenhair fern, are used in large quantities to create a look that is graceful without being stark. The elegant wedding-flower designs are strengthened by limiting the types of flower used, and the lilies' delicious scent will be remembered by the happy couple and their guests for years to come.

A single stem of longiflorum lily matches the graceful elegance of the wedding dress. The stem is treated in a stylised way with two extra buds bound to a main stem that is left long to accentuate the line and fall of the dress. The bridesmaid carries a posy of maidenhair fern, lily-of-the-valley and tiny rosebuds. On her head she wears a headband of delicate lily-of-the-valley and rosebuds that is held securely in place by ends that fit over her bunches.

Long satin gloves are the perfect accessory for a simple dress and elegant lily stem.

ALTERNATIVES

Calla lilies or any oriental hybrid lily would be a good choice. Trailing ivy makes an acceptable alternative to fern.

A stone urn is filled with a profusion of longiflorum lilies, their stems left long to create the effect that they are growing. The lilies are ringed with maidenhair fern that froths over the top of the urn. Developing the floral theme, church flowers combine longiflorum lilies and maidenhair fern, nestling under a lovely stone carving of a dove (see opposite).

The floral theme for this elegant wedding centres around the shape of the open longiflorum lily, which has been used to great effect for the centrepieces. Single lily heads are placed in trumpet-shaped glasses filled with water. A number of glasses is grouped in the centre of each guest table.

ASSEMBLY DETAILS

One stem of longiflorum lily is chosen for the **bouquet** and each flower and bud is externally wired with 22 gauge (0.71 mm) wire. Extra buds are added by first wiring then binding them with florist's pot tape. A small amount of white ribbon, 1 cm (½ in) wide, is used to finish off the binding point. For the **lily urn**, a large bowl is filled with plastic foam and placed inside the urn. The stems of longiflorum lilies are pushed into the foam to create a column of flowers. Pieces of cane 30 cm (12 in) in length are pushed through the hole in the bottom of each pot of maidenhair fern, which is then spiked into the foam to anchor the pot in place. Moss is pushed between the fern fronds to cover the pots and complete the design. The arrangements decorating the **church entrance** are made by externally wiring the lilies and attaching them to the rim of the maidenhair fern pots. The pots are then suspended from the stone carvings with 22 gauge (0.71 mm) wire.

PLANT MATERIAL

Lilium longiflorum
Longiflorum lily

Adiantum
Maidenhair fern

Convallaria majalis
Lily-of-the-valley

Rosa
Miniature roses

DESIGN RECIPE

Bouquet:
2 lily stems

Lily urn:
20 lily stems
5 maidenhair fern plants

Church entrance:
2 lily stems
2 maidenhair fern plants

Bridesmaid's posy:
1 maidenhair fern plant
10 lily-of-the-valley stems
2 white miniature rose stems

Bridesmaid's headband:
10 lily-of-the-valley stems
6 miniature roses

Each centrepiece:
The number of stems required
   will depend on how many
   flowers are open, but 3 stems
   should be sufficient for one
   centrepiece

A small wet foam holder is used as the base for the **bridesmaid's posy**, with foliage and flowers simply pushed into the foam, the foliage attached first to create a framework. For the **bridesmaid's headband**, lily-of-the-valley is first support-wired with 30 gauge (0.32 mm) wire, mounted onto a 28 gauge (0.38 mm) silver wire then taped with florist's corsage tape. Small rosebuds are wired with a 24 gauge (0.56 mm) wire and taped. A 20 gauge (0.90 mm) wire, approximately 28 cm (11 in) in length, is taped with corsage tape. The individual flowers are then layered and taped onto this wire, alternating 1 or 2 stems of lily-of-the-valley with 1 rosebud until the required length is created.

TIP Remove all stamens from open lilies so that they cannot stain clothes.

The cake is raised on a white
organza-covered box so that it
appears to float above a bed of
gorgeous flowers.

An arch of soft lilac and pink flowers decorates the
limestone walls of the church entrance. Guests will
immediately appreciate the care and attention you
have taken to set the scene (opposite page).

A MEDLEY OF BLOOMS
Roses, Stocks and Delphiniums

Fine summer weather brings with it the possibility of celebrating a wedding outdoors. Open-air settings require themes that link the occasion to the place and time of year and a garden with a well-kept lawn bordered with flowering shrubs cries out for arrangements that emphasise the country feel. Summer provides a wide range of pretty flowers, and here those in subtle pinks, lilacs, ivories and white blend with one another to create a delightful combination of soft textures and heady fragrances.

Arriving at this old country church (above), guests are greeted by an arch of blooms over the lovely doorway. Dappled sunlight filters through the trees in the churchyard, bringing out the patina in the studded oak door. This style of arranging depends on blending a number of flower types so that colours flow in a gentle rhythm. Stepping back and looking at the whole arch, the effect is very soft with pockets of deeper tones that hold the eye a little longer than the rest. The design is finished at the base with two urns from which the whole arch appears to spring upwards and the arrangement provides a wonderful backdrop for photographs (see overleaf).

Summer sunshine brings golden light to this flower-bedecked canopy in an idyllic garden setting (opposite page).

The canopy in the garden has carved wooden supports painted with a white marbled finish and cream-coloured fabric edged with a pearl trim. It is positioned so that the shrubs bordering the lawn may be glimpsed through it, which allows the whole garden to play its part in setting the scene. Massed flowers decorate the top and bottom of each of the canopy poles, with the centre of each pole and the fabric top to the canopy are lightly wound around with ruscus (see pages 98 and 99). The soft colours of the flower groupings pick out the colours of the rhododendrons in the background shrubbery.

The decorations at the foot of the poles not only add visual weight to the overall effect but also help disguise the metal supports anchoring the poles to the ground.

Lilies, hydrangeas, delphiniums, stocks and Texas bluebells vie for attention in this celebration of the English garden (left).

A medley of summer blooms enhances the corners of the canopy and adds to the festive feel (left).

Groups of flowers at the base of each pole (right) are both decorative and practical, concealing as they do the metal foot supports.

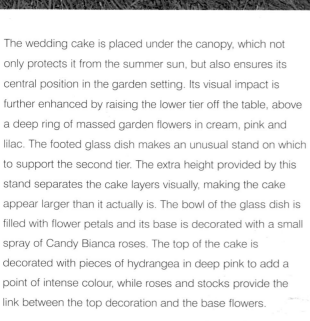

The wedding cake is placed under the canopy, which not only protects it from the summer sun, but also ensures its central position in the garden setting. Its visual impact is further enhanced by raising the lower tier off the table, above a deep ring of massed garden flowers in cream, pink and lilac. The footed glass dish makes an unusual stand on which to support the second tier. The extra height provided by this stand separates the cake layers visually, making the cake appear larger than it actually is. The bowl of the glass dish is filled with flower petals and its base is decorated with a small spray of Candy Bianca roses. The top of the cake is decorated with pieces of hydrangea in deep pink to add a point of intense colour, while roses and stocks provide the link between the top decoration and the base flowers.

The open flowers of Le Rêve lilies in lilac pink make a beautiful, tightly packed posy-style bouquet. For an unusual effect reflecting the detail on the bodice, each of the open lilies has pearls fixed to its centre, taking the place of its pollen sac. Open flowers are used without any foliage for this bouquet, the effect being light and delicate. The English summer garden feel is carried through to the mother-of-the-bride's hat decoration, its pale pink Candy Bianca roses blending wonderfully with the lavender dress coat.

PLANT MATERIAL

Rosa 'Candy Bianca'
Candy Bianca rose

Lilium 'Le Rêve'
Le Rêve lily

Eustoma grandiflorum
Texas bluebell

Matthiola incana Anthony and
Cleopatra series
Stock

Hydrangea macrophylla
Hydrangea

Lathyrus odoratus
Sweet pea

Delphinium 'Pacific Giant'
Pacific Giant delphinium

Saponaria
Soapwort

Amaranthus caudatus
Love-lies-bleeding

Eucalyptus
Eucalyptus

Hedera
Ivy

Alchemilla mollis
Lady's mantle

Ruscus aculeatus
Butcher's broom

DESIGN RECIPE

Church arch:

10 hydrangea heads

40 roses

20 lily stems

20 delphiniums

40 stocks

40 Texas bluebell stems

6 love-lies-bleeding stems

3 bunches eucalyptus

30 to 40 pieces ivy to fill

Each top canopy arrangement:

3 lily stems

5 stocks

1 full stem soapwort

2 love-lies-bleeding stems

3 Texas bluebell stems

**Each bottom canopy
arrangement:**

4 lily stems

5 stocks

3 delphiniums

4 Texas bluebell stems

Each canopy pole:

4 pieces ruscus

Base ring for cake:

15 roses

10 Texas bluebell stems

10 stocks

2 delphiniums

4 lady's mantle stems

Glass support for cake:

2 roses

1 Texas bluebell

3 roses, 1 stock, ½ hydrangea
    head for petals

Cake top arrangement:

½ hydrangea head

6 roses

3 stocks

Bouquet:

15 to 16 lily flower heads

Hat decoration:

3 roses

ASSEMBLY DETAILS

The floral **church arch** is based on a wooden frame, made to the size of the doorway. Seven blocks of wet foam are attached to the frame to act as a moist anchor for the flowers and foliage. The flowers are inserted into the foam and, a few hours before the wedding, the frame is attached to the wall. Wet foam is also used as a base for the **canopy flowers**. Small flat plastic dishes containing wet foam are placed at the foot of the canopy poles and filled with flowers. An additional set of dishes is suspended from the top corners of the canopy with wire and filled with flowers in a light, flowing style. Pieces of ruscus are pinned to the canopy along its edges and around the supporting poles. For the **cake**, a wet foam wreath ring 40 cm (16 in) in diameter is filled with flowers and placed on top of a solid box covered with white organza. The cake is positioned within the wreath so that it looks as if it is resting on a bed of flowers. The glass support for the top tier is decorated with a wired corsage of roses attached to the stand with fine ribbon. The bowl is filled with petals and the top tier placed on the stand. A very small white plastic container holding wet foam provides the base for the top arrangement. Since this is being placed directly on the icing, the base of the container is kept very clean and dry.

To make the **bouquet**, the stamens are removed from individual lily heads and wired pearls are pushed into the base of the flower where all the petals meet. Each lily head is then support-wired with a 22 gauge (0.71 mm) wire inserted into the head and externally wired around the stem. The support wires are all cut to approximately 8 cm (3 in) and, starting from the middle and working outwards, the individual flower heads are inserted into a wet foam holder, each flower touching the next to achieve a tightly packed look. For the **hat decoration**, three roses are each wired with a 22 gauge (0.71 mm) wire through the base of the stem then taped with florist's corsage tape. The three roses are formed into a corsage by layering them slightly and binding them with 28 gauge (0.38 mm) binding wire as close to the base of the roses as possible. The resulting wire stem is cut to length and taped. The whole corsage is then tied with fine ribbon and attached to the base of the hat brim close to the crown, using the organza decoration on the hat as an anchoring point.

ALTERNATIVES
Peonies, larkspur, camellias, rhododendrons, African blue lilies and – later in the season – dahlias would all be suitable alternatives.

A SYMPHONY OF SCENTS
Peonies, Tuberose and Lilacs

Scent is often the aspect of a floral arrangement that lingers in the memory the longest, so when selecting wedding flowers, always be aware of the perfume that flowers can add to an occasion. It is often not the brightest or biggest blooms that have the strongest scents, but bold flowers can be combined with more subtle and delicate flowers and foliages that have wonderful perfume. Here a delicious combination of scents creates a truly romantic feel.

An attractive way of setting the scene and letting guests know they have arrived at the correct place is to decorate the church gate with a welcome wreath of flowers. The wreath is made from the massed heads of the snowball bush and the top and bottom of the wreath are finished with groups of white peonies and white silk bows. Inside the church, a wild, flowing arrangement in white and ivory is set on a windowsill. Groups of delphiniums, tuberose and snowball bush make up the outer framework of the display, while mock orange stems pour over the windowsil and fill the space with fragrance..

Arrangements of simple garden flowers with exquisite perfumes fill this little country church with a heady mix of scents.

A hand-tied spray bouquet suits the simplicity of the bride's gown. Stems of tuberose are layered with pieces of mock orange and trails of delicate stephanotis, while double peonies add some bolder forms. The tiara headdress combines flowers from a stem of tuberose with sparkly crystals so that the fine veil may be seen through the tracery of flowers, crystals and silver wire.

This tuberose-and-crystal tiara headdress looks light and delicate, and is a stunning piece for any bride to wear.

The bridesmaids' hand-tied posies are in muted raspberry and soft pink tones. Like the bride, the bridesmaids are dressed in white, but their more colourful posies provide a fitting contrast to the pale bridal bouquet. The mother-of-the-bride wears a pretty wristlet that follows the style of the bride's tiara headdress with its inclusion of crystals and tuberoses.

PLANT MATERIAL

Paeonia
Peony

Philadelphus
Mock orange

Polianthes tuberosa
Tuberose

Stephanotis
Stephanotis

Viburnum opulus
Snowball bush

Delphinium New Century hybrids
New Century delphinium

Alstroemeria aurantiaca
Peruvian lily

Astrantia major
Masterwort

Lunaria
Honesty

Campanula persicifolia
Campanula

Syringa
White lilac

ALTERNATIVES
Any of the highly perfumed flowers of early- to mid-summer, including a whole range of lilies and many of the early summer roses, would be wonderful.

A delicate floral wristlet is an
alternative to a corsage. Here,
masterwort and tuberose combine
beautifully with oyster-coloured
disks of dried honesty and crystals.

DESIGN RECIPE

Welcome wreath:

30 to 40 snowball bush heads

5 peonies

Church window arrangement:

5 peonies

10 tuberose stems

10 delphinium stems

6 snowball bush stems

6 mock orange stems

5 campanula stems

4 lilac stems

Bouquet:

5 peonies

7 tuberose stems

1 stephanotis plant

3 mock orange stems

Tiara headdress:

2 tuberose stems

10 wired crystals

Bridesmaid's posy:

3 Peruvian lily stems

7 masterwort stems

Wristlet:

1 tuberose stem

1 masterwort stem

5 honesty disks

6 wired crystals

ASSEMBLY DETAILS

For the **welcome wreath**, a 40 cm (16 in) plastic foam wreath ring is soaked in flower food solution. Individual heads of snowball bush are support-mounted on 22 gauge (0.71 mm) wire and cut to about 8 cm (3 in). They are then pushed into the plastic foam to create a domed ring of heads. Large peony flowers are added at the top and bottom of the wreath and ribbon bows complete the design. The **church window arrangement** is based on wet foam that has been soaked in flower food solution and anchored into a deep plastic bowl large enough to take the required stems and still allow a good reservoir of water. This is then covered with wire mesh and taped into position. Lighter, longer flower stems are added to the back and sides with bolder and shorter material added to the front and centre. Transitional material is added as required to create a flowing effect, allowing every flower to be seen in its own space.

The flower and foliage stems for the **bouquet** are organised according to stem length and flower size, the lighter stems to be used on the outside of the bouquet and the bolder, more open flowers to be placed in the centre and down towards the handle. All the flower stems are prepared by stripping the leaves below the estimated binding point for each stem. A strong flower stem is taken first and more stems are added to it in a layered fashion. The handle is taped and the binding point covered and wrapped with ribbon 5 cm (2 in) wide. For the **tiara headdress**, 17 to 20 florets of tuberose are wired individually on 28 gauge (0.38 mm) silver stub wires and taped with florist's white corsage tape. A 20 gauge (0.90 mm) stay wire is also taped with white corsage tape. The single wired florets of tuberose are taped to the stay wire in a layered fashion, alternating with wired crystals. The length of the headdress should be about 13 to 15 cm (5 to 6 in). The whole piece is sewn onto a hair comb ready to be pushed into the hair next to the veil.

The stems for the **bridesmaid's posy** are prepared by removing all the foliage. The three stems of Peruvian lily are arranged in a teepee shape created at the point where the individual stems branch. This creates a framework for the delicate masterwort stems to be positioned at the same height between the Peruvian lilies. Stems should be added one at a time from the same direction, turning the posy as required to create an even distribution of flowers. The posy is wrapped with tape and finally tied with ribbon. For the floral **wristlet,** each flower is individually wired onto a 28 gauge (0.38 mm) stub wire and taped. Then, flowers of the same kind are taped together and these flower clusters of 2 or 3 are grouped around the central wired-and-taped masterwort flowers. The wired crystals are added to the sides and small pieces of honesty glued under the central flower to cover the binding point. The whole arrangement is tied to the wrist with fine ribbon.

The bridesmaids carry a floral rope of box
foliage, ranunculus and lily-of-the-valley.

PURELY ELEGANT
Lily-of-the-Valley and Ranunculus

One of the most striking of all flower combinations is white and green, producing as it does an elegance that few other colour palettes can match. If more unusual flowers are combined in this way, the effect can be truly original and fresh. For this floral theme, creamy white ranunculus, lily-of-the-valley, Solomon's seal and foliage of brachyglottis combine in a fusion of light and airy flowers and stems.

A hand-tied posy of lily-of-the-valley and ranunculus looks beautiful with a simple wedding dress. The delicately layered curves of the white ranunculus petals echo the soft, draping folds of the silk chiffon on the front of the dress, while the slightly furry grey-green leaves of brachyglottis add substance and separate the individual flowers, allowing their shapes to be seen. The crescent-shaped headdress complements the posy by grouping ranunculus heads with lily-of-the-valley flowers and is placed at the back of the hair, just catching the veil (see overleaf).

Giving two young bridesmaids a floral rope to carry as they follow the bride down the aisle is a delightful way to arrange their flowers. White satin handles make the piece easy for children to hold, and each bridesmaid wears a light garland headdress of lily-of-the-valley, tied at the back with a bow of satin ribbon.

The unusual centrepieces (see page 113) allow the pretty silver mesh that holds up the flowers to become an integral part of the design . The flowers are arranged in roughly three layers, with short heads of ranunculus placed low in the arrangement, open flowers on longer stems adding height and wispy stems of Solomon's seal with ranunculus buds on long stems forming the highest element of the design.

The slim-line dress of silk overlaid with chiffon has a very young and feminine appeal, complemented by the ranunculus and delicate spikes of lily-of-the-valley in the bouquet.

The headdress anchors the veil securely and beautifully, allowing the bride to feel confident during the ceremony.

Lily-of-the-valley adds a wonderful perfume to the elegant bouquet.

ASSEMBLY DETAILS

The **bride's bouquet** is based on a wet foam holder, with stems cut to length and inserted into the dampened foam. The brachyglottis foliage is added first, followed by ranunculus flowers and small clusters of lily-of-the-valley. For the **bride's headdress**, the ranunculus stems are cut to about 8 cm (3 in) below the flower heads and a 24 gauge (0.56 mm) wire is pushed into each stem and up into the head. The stem is cross-plied with a 28 gauge (0.38 mm) silver wire then taped. The lily-of-the-valley pieces are also wired and taped. Some of the pieces of lily-of-the-valley are taped to a 20 gauge (0.90 mm) stay wire about 15 cm (6 in) in length. Two of the ranunculus flowers are added at the base. This is repeated and the two halves joined together. The remaining two pieces of ranunculus are wired to the top and bottom of the central join and the headdress is attached to a comb with fine wire.

To gauge the length for the **floral rope**, the two bridesmaids must stand together at approximately the same distance they will be when walking in front of the bride. If they hold a length of string or rope between them to form a gentle curve, the bottom at least 25 cm (10 in) from the floor, this will give a length for the floral rope, including ribbon handles. A length of medium-thickness rope or 1 cm (½-in) diameter flexible plastic pipe is used for the base. Each of the ranunculus flowers is wired internally with a 22 gauge (0.71 mm) wire and cross-plied with a 28 gauge (0.38 mm) silver wire. Bunches of lily-of-the-valley are wired on 28 gauge (0.38 mm) wires. Box foliage, lily-of-the-valley and ranunculus are then taped to the base in a layered manner until it is completely covered. For the **bridesmaids' headdresses**, a length of headdress wire is cut to size for the base of each garland and the pieces of lily-of-the-valley are wired onto 28 gauge (0.38 mm) stub wires. Starting at one end, the pieces of lily-of-the-valley are taped to the headdress wire in a layered fashion, keeping them in a thin line. When the required length is reached, the ends are taped together to close the garland. Each headdress is finished with a bow of white ribbon.

The construction of the **centrepiece** relies on two pieces of silver wire mesh the right size to fit in a shallow glass bowl. Both pieces are pressed into the shape of the bowl, then one of these is inverted over the other and secured to create a domed frame. This is then placed in the dish and the flower stems are held securely by being passed through both layers of mesh and into the water below.

TIP Remove the leaves from Solomon's seal to reveal the delicate flowers that hide under them.

Tables at the wedding reception are decorated with combinations of ranunculus, lily-of-the-valley and Solomon's seal arranged in a shallow glass dish.

PLANT MATERIAL

Ranunculus asiaticus
Ranunculus

Convallaria majalis
Lily-of-the-valley

Buxus sempervirens
Box

Polygonatum
Solomon's seal

Brachyglottis
Brachyglottis

DESIGN RECIPE

Bride's bouquet:
10 open ranunculus heads
25 to 30 pieces lily-of-the-valley
9 or 10 pieces brachyglottis
  foliage

Bride's headdress:
6 ranunculus heads
10 pieces lily-of-the-valley

Bridesmaids' floral rope:
2 bunches box foliage
9 ranunculus heads
15 pieces lily-of-the-valley

Bridesmaids' garland headdresses:
25 to 30 pieces lily-of-the-valley

Each centrepiece:
12 to 15 ranunculus stems
  with buds
10 to 15 pieces lily-of-the-valley
5 pieces Solomon's seal

LAVENDER BLUE,
LAVENDER GREEN
Lavender and Sweet Peas

Heady fragrance emanates from this lavender-covered basket filled with fresh flower petals.

Fragrance abounds in this mixture of scented garden flowers. Lavender and sweet peas form the basis of the floral theme with other fragrant summer flowers making an appearance throughout. Shades of blue, lilac and purple form a floral combination that looks wonderfully bright and rich on a sunny day. In the gorgeous garden setting, the white bouvardia in the bouquet repeats the accents of white in the linen, chairs and canopy walls.

Fragrance is a very important factor in the bouquet and the mingling scents of lavender and sweet peas creates a heady mix. To accompany the nosegay-style bouquet, a simple garland headdress is placed over the veil to anchor it in place. Wicker baskets are bound with lavender and filled to the brim with fragrant petals to be thrown as natural confetti after the ceremony. Sweet pea and rose petals are combined with fresh lavender stripped from the spike to give a wonderful mixture of summer scents.

Tied with a delicate lilac chiffon ribbon, the blues and whites of the bride's posy evoke the summer sky.

The white cake on an antique lace tablecloth set against white voile drapes looks fresh and inviting on a hot day. Touches of blue and lavender spiralling around each tier are created by laying flower heads end to end along the edge of each cake board. Sage flowers are laid on the bottom tier, rich purple brodiaea flowers are arranged around the middle tier and African blue lily flowers are placed around the top tier, with a mixture of the flowers forming the top decoration.

Mixed fragrant blooms in shades of purple, lilac and blue form the basis of the ties for the canopy drapes. Campanula, love-in-a-mist and eucalyptus foliage join the perfumed garden flowers to create luscious arrangements.

Set on an antique lace tablecloth, the three-tier wedding cake is decorated simply but effectively with rings of flower heads in different shades of blue (left).

Floral arrangements on the tables that are spread across the lawn are placed around the base of tall, stemmed glass bowls containing medium-sized pillar candles. When the candles are lit, their warmth will encourage the flowers to give off even more of their lovely perfume. The white slatted chairs (see page 119) are decorated with a small bunch of sweet peas and lavender and, as guests brush past, the scents will fill the air . As the light fades and the evening celebrations progress, floral lanterns hung in trees are lit and add a magic of their own to the occasion (see page 121).

For the reception, round tables covered with white linen tablecloths are placed throughout the garden and decorated with delicate and fragrant arrangements.

White embroidered napkins set on pale blue-and-white patterned plates are decorated with bunches of country flowers that show off the contrast between the white cake and and the simple flower decoration on each tier.

Small bunches of fragrant garden flowers tied with ribbon not only look delightful set against the white chairs (opposite), but are ready to release their scent when brushed by passers-by.

ASSEMBLY DETAILS

The stems for the **bouquet** are cut to length and stripped of their leaves below the estimated binding point. A strong stem is chosen for the centre of the bouquet and all the other stems are spiralled around it, then bound with tape. Two ribbon bows cover the binding point. For the **headdress**, individual flowers are wired on 28 gauge (0.38 mm) silver wires and taped with green corsage tape. The wired flowers are taped to a 19 gauge (1.0 mm) wire with a small space between each until the required length is reached and the ends of the wire are then taped together.

The **lavender baskets** are created by binding the edges of shallow wicker baskets with sprigs of lavender using 28 gauge (0.38 mm) silver binding wire. The handle of the basket is bound with ribbon 2.5 cm (1 in) wide. Lavender is bound to this too. The flower heads are pulled apart carefully so as not to damage the petals, and larger petals are placed at the bottom of the basket with more delicate petals on top.

For the **cake decoration**, individual flowers are laid end to end along the edge of the cake board, each tier having a different flower type. A small mound of flowers is laid on the top. The basis of the **curtain decorations** is a shallow plastic container filled with wet foam, secured with florist's pot tape. A piece of ribbon is tied to the tape at the edge of the container ready to attach the arrangement to the curtain. The outer framework of foliage and flowers is pushed into the foam, followed by the flowers in the centre. Just before the decoration is hung on the curtain, the container is tipped over to allow any excess water to drain away and not stain the fabric.

For the **napkin ties,** a small group of flowers is formed into a bunch by placing the finer, longer stems to the back and rounder, shorter stems to the front. The bunch is then tied to the napkins with fine bootlace ribbon.

Lavender, sweet peas and brodiaea are tied into a bunch with tape to form the basis of the **chairback decorations**. Each bunch is placed in a shallow container of flower food solution. Ribbon bows with long ties are made; and just before the ceremony, the flower bunches are taken out of the water and the ribbon is tied to them and then to the chairs. For the **centrepieces**, a shallow plastic dish is filled with plastic foam cut level with the rim of the dish. The glass dish is placed on the foam and flowers inserted into it around the base. The bowl of the dish is then lined with foliage and a piece of foam is placed in the centre. Flowers are pushed into the foam, leaving the centre clear for the candle. For extra security, wires 2.5 cm (1 in) in length are taped to the bottom of the candle and the candle is spiked into the foam.

The **lantern decoration** is based on a small plastic dish suspended slightly below the lantern. Very small holes are drilled into the rim of the dish and fine wire pushed through them to attach the dish to the lantern base. Wet foam is secured to the dish, and flowers and foliage are then pushed into the foam to form a pretty wreath.

PLANT MATERIAL

Bouvardia longiflora
 'White Charla'
White Charla bouvardia

Lavandula angustifolia
 'Munstead'
Munstead lavender

Lavandula stoechas
French lavender

Lathyrus odoratus 'Lord Nelson'
Lord Nelson sweet pea

Lathyrus odoratus 'Liz Taylor'
Liz Taylor sweet pea

Agapanthus
African blue lily

Brodiaea
Brodiaea

Campanula
Campanula

Nigella
Love-in-a-mist

Eucalyptus
Eucalyptus

Salvia
Sage

Rosa 'Candy Bianca'
Candy Bianca rose

Scabiosa
Scabiosa

TIP If using flower heads to decorate the cake, choose flowers that will last well out of water. The later they can be arranged around the cake, the fresher they will look.

DESIGN RECIPE

Bouquet:

3 bouvardia stems

20 to 30 lavender stems

20 sweet pea stems

Headdress:

15 Lord Nelson sweet pea buds

1 bouvardia stem

12 sprigs lavender

15 African blue lily pips

6 heads love-in-a-mist

Each lavender basket:

1 bunch lavender
   (approximately 60 stems)

4 roses (or enough petals to
   fill the basket)

10 lavender sprigs, stripped

30 to 40 sweet pea stems

Bottom tier of the cake:

30 sage flowers

Middle tier of the cake:

25 brodiaea flowers

Top tier of the cake:

15 African blue lily flowers

10 mixed flowers for the top
   decoration

Each drape decoration:

2 campanula stems

10 sweet pea stems

2 scabiosa stems

20 lavender stems

2 branched eucalyptus stems

Each napkin ring:

5 lavender sprigs

3 brodiaea heads

Each chairback decoration:

5 lavender sprigs

3 to 5 sweet pea stems

1 brodiaea stem

Each centrepiece:

15 to 20 lavender sprigs

1 campanula stem

1 well-branched eucalyptus stem

10 sweet pea stems

5 love-in-a-mist stems

Each lantern decoration:

10 lavender stems

10 sweet pea stems

2 eucalyptus stems

5 love-in-a-mist stems

section four…

floral facts

care and conditioning

Wedding flowers need to look their best for the occasion and this means preparing them properly, whether they be shop bought or picked from the garden. The lasting qualities of commercially produced flowers have improved greatly over the last few years due to considerable research into the best time to cut them, but they will still need conditioning when you get them home. The method of conditioning will vary according to the type of flower and to its intended use, but by following a few simple rules, you can ensure that the flowers you have chosen will be in optimum condition on the big day.

GENERAL CARE OF CUT-FLOWER MATERIAL

When cutting flowers from the garden, do so during the coolest parts of the day, which is usually during the early morning or in the late evening. At these times, the transpiration rate of plant material (the amount of water lost by the leaves and flowers by evaporation) is at its lowest. The same applies when buying flowers. Do not buy flowers during the warmest part of the day unless they are in water and in the shade, and do not leave them in hot places such as a car for any longer than necessary. Stress of this kind can reduce the vase life of cut flowers by up to 50 percent.

As soon as you get the flowers home from the shop or in from the garden, remove any outer packaging and strip off the lower leaves and any damaged petals. Recut the stem ends (see 'Cutting Stems' below) and place the flowers in tepid water for at least two hours before use. There are a number of special conditioning techniques for different stem structures that are discussed in detail later in this section.

Cutting stems

Most people cut stems with a pair of scissors or pruning shears. Using a sharp knife, however, will minimise damage to the stem cells, as a blade does not squeeze the stems and rupture the cells at the sides. Stems should be cut at an angle to expose the largest possible surface area of cells, thus allowing the maximum uptake of water.

Recutting the stems is best done underwater, as this prevents an air lock from forming and so aids the free flow of water and nutrients up the stem. Choose a deep bucket or bowl that is wide enough to hold both your hand and a knife. Fill the bucket with water, place the stems to be cut in it, and cut off about 2.5 cm (1 in) of the stem end.

Conditioning time

Let flowers and foliage condition for at least two hours in a cool place before using them. This will allow the stems to take up the maximum amount of water and extend their vase life. Adding cut-flower food to the water will help the cells swell. It will also help keep the water clean, as it contains a fungicide

that kills bacteria. After about two hours, quickly transfer the plant material to the display container, keeping the stem ends wet to prevent air locks forming.

Direct sources of heat

Hot, dry conditions, which are often found in hotels and banquet halls, can increase the transpiration rate of plant material, drying out delicate petals and reducing the vase life of cut flowers. Place fresh flowers and leaves as far away as possible from radiators and other sources of heat. Keep them away from south-facing windows, where the sun shining through the glass can cause very warm conditions.

Bacteria

Bacteria that affect cut flowers and leaves are caused by decaying plant material in the water. This can be seen very clearly in a glass vase when, after about two days, the water starts to become cloudy as the bacteria develop and multiply. Cloudy water may look unsightly but the main effect of this build up of bacteria is to block the vessels and water-carrying cells of the flower stems and prevent the uptake of water and essential nutrients. As a result, flowers and leaves will wilt prematurely and buds or half-open flowers will not develop fully.

To avoid the development of bacteria, make sure that all containers are washed and free from bacteria before using them. Rinsing the container is not enough, particularly if it is a favourite one that is in constant use. Glass containers only look attractive when clean, but pottery or other opaque containers can often be overlooked. Use a brush to remove any residue from rims or the bottom of the container. Remove any leaves from the bottom of flower or leaf stems that are below the water level. Plant material submerged in water will start to rot and so increase the incidence of bacteria forming in the water. To keep the vase water as clean as possible, add either a flower food containing a fungicide or a small amount of bleach (two or three drops should suffice for a medium-sized vase), both of which will prevent bacteria developing.

Ethylene

Ethylene is an odourless gas produced by all plants, flowers, leaves and fruit as they age; and its presence speeds up the aging process. Ethylene levels can also increase when a plant or flower is damaged or stressed. In the case of cut flowers, the largest amount of the gas is emitted by the calyx of the flower, the part below the petals that would later form the seedpod. The rate that a flower produces the gas naturally is a good indicator of its vase-life potential. Ethylene-sensitive flowers include sweet peas, most species of carnations (dianthus), freesias, Peruvian lilies and roses.

Many commercial growers are now able to treat these flowers to slow down the production of ethylene. These pretreated flowers can last up to 50 or 60 percent longer in the vase than untreated ones. Since fruit also exudes ethylene, it is best not to leave fruit and cut flowers in the same room. A combination of certain fruit such as bananas and susceptible flowers such as carnations can be very dramatic, with the flowers withering and aging overnight. Other effects of the gas are yellowing of leaves, leaf drop and the failure of buds to open.

STEM STRUCTURES AND CONDITIONING METHODS

Cut flowers display a range of stem types and the conditioning methods vary accordingly. Warm-water conditioning is the most common method; but sometimes boiling water is used and occasionally the stem ends are sealed with a flame. It is useful to look at these methods in terms of the stem type so that it becomes a simple matter to choose the best method to maximise the vase life of cut flowers.

Soft stems: warm-water conditioning

Most spring flowers such as tulips, grape hyacinths and daffodils have soft stems. The latter exude a sticky sap and should always be conditioned and displayed separately from other flowers: Peruvian lilies, anemones and gerberas are other popular soft-stemmed flowers.

The warm-water method is very effective with this type of stem. Fill a bucket or wide-based container with about 8 cm (3 in) of warm water – if the water is too hot for your hand, it is too hot for the flower stems. Leave the stems in this water for about five minutes and then fill the bucket about one-third the way up the stems with cold water so that the final temperature is tepid. Leave the flowers to condition in this water for at least two hours before using.

Firm stems: warm-water conditioning

These types of flowers include carnations, a number of cut-flower orchids, chrysanthemums and a whole range of herbaceous flowers easily grown in the garden. Conditioning in warm water suits these stems, as heated water is taken up the stem more rapidly, reducing the possibility of an air lock in the stem. If too many air bubbles occur, the flow of water is restricted and the flower head will wilt.

Woody stems: boiling-water conditioning

Boiling water is required when dealing with woody stems, including outdoor-grown chrysanthemums, herbaceous flowers such as Michaelmas daisies and most trees and shrubs. Before starting this method, make sure the flower heads and young leaves are protected with tissue or other paper, as this will prevent damage to the flowers from the rising steam.

Fill a container that will withstand the heat with 2.5 to 5 cm (1 to 2 in) boiling water. Cut each flower or foliage stem with a sharp knife at a long oblique angle and immediately plunge the stem end into the water. Leave the stems in this water for up to one minute and then fill the container with cold water until the water is tepid. Leave the stems to condition in a cool place out of direct heat for up to two hours. Flower food suitable for woody stems can also be added.

Hollow stems: plugging method

There are a number of plants, such as delphiniums, lupins and dahlias, that have hollow stems. When cut, these flowers sometimes find it difficult to take up water. A very effective (though time-consuming) method of conditioning these flowers is to invert each stem, fill it with cool or tepid water and plug the end with a tissue, cotton ball, or anything that will act as a wick. Place the filled stems right way up in about 6 to 8 in (15 to 20 cm) of tepid water. This will allow the flowers to develop fully and last much longer.

Latex-producing stems: boiling-water or searing method

There are various plants that produce a milky or latex-type sap when cut. The most common cut flowers of this type are euphorbias, but poppies and rubber plant foliage require the same treatment. Wear gloves when handling these stems because some people have an allergic reaction if the sap comes in contact with their skin.

Latex-producing stems can be conditioned effectively using the boiling-water method, but they can also be treated by searing the end of each stem over the flame of either a candle, a match, or a small gas burner. To do this, quickly pass the stem end through the flame, rotating it to make sure all sides are seared and then immediately place it in tepid water.

Special technique

In some of the arrangements described in this book, flowers have been laid across bowls and other containers: an unusual and evocative way of creating a feeling or mood. Certain flowers will last out of water better than others, especially if properly conditioned. Calla lilies, for example, will last out of water for up to ten days if the stem end is completely sealed with florist's glue. By preventing air from entering the stem, evaporation of water from the stem end is reduced and the flower is able to use the water already trapped in the stem.

The 'Special technique' described
above enables arrangements such
as this to
stay fresh for days.

materials and techniques

This section is designed to stimulate interest in experimenting with floristry techniques. I hope the step-by-step photographs will give you the confidence to reproduce arrangements that may look complex but are, in fact, easy to make once you know how.

On the following pages, you will find examples of both the basic and the more complex wiring techniques employed in the making of the designs in this book. You will also find information on such things as using natural stems as containers for other flowers. If you want to learn more about new floristry styles or even become a florist, ask at your local adult education department about courses in your area. The important thing is to enjoy experimenting with flowers and foliage.

Tools and equipment

Certain basic tools and equipment are essential when starting out in floristry. By far, the most important of these are tools for cutting stems and wire. A good pair of scissors that will cut florist's wire is essential, as is a sharp knife for flower stems. Florist's corsage tape in white and green and white or green pot tape to secure foam into containers is also useful. These items, along with a range of wires in various gauges, are all you need for wedding floristry. Also illustrated are foam bouquet holders and the decorative reel wires used in many modern floristry techniques; while not essential, they will increase your range. They are used to create projects in this book.

In the top row (left to right) are: wet foam block, white pot tape, a range of florist's corsage tape, green pot tape, stem fix, decorative pearls; middle row (left to right): decorative cord, ribbon, scissors, reel wire in various gauges; bottom row (left to right): scissors, knife, florist's stub wires in various lengths and gauges, wet foam bouquet holders.

BASIC WIRING TECHNIQUES

Loop stitch and making units

This technique is very useful for corsage, buttonhole and headdress designs.

1 Feed a florist's 32 gauge (0.28 mm) silver stub wire from the back of the leaf through to the front then back again, trapping the centre rib of the leaf with the wire loop. Holding the wire and the centre rib of the leaf between the forefinger and thumb of one hand, ease the two ends of the wire downwards with the other hand until they meet.

2 Still holding the wire and leaf in one hand, wrap one end of the wire around the stem and the other length of wire, binding them together. This will support the leaf and give it a strong stem.

3 Using florist's corsage tape of the required colour, place the cut end behind the wired stem and hold it in place with your forefinger. Then rotate the leaf, pulling the tape at the same time, so that it sticks to itself as it winds down the stem.

4 Individually taped leaves can then be assembled into units of two and three leaves. To achieve a natural-looking result, make sure there is a gap of about 6 mm (¼ in) between the top tip of the second leaf and the base of the first. This will give you a well-balanced unit.

> **TAPE** Florist's corsage tape is a slightly sticky paper tape and the easiest kind to use. However, finer results can be achieved with plastic tapes or by cutting the corsage tape in half widthwise. This should only be done once you have mastered the technique of using the full width.

External wiring technique

This technique is used to support hard stems, particularly those of roses. It is used for the rose bouquet on page 19.

1 Steady the flower with one hand and with the other hand, push a 22 gauge (0.71 mm) wire into its calyx.

2 Using both hands, twist the stem and the wire so that the wire travels in a spiral down the stem.

Wiring a flower head without a stem

This method is used for buttonholes, corsages, headdresses and wired bridal bouquets.

1 Cut off the flower head, leaving about 6 mm (¼ in) of stem at the base of the calyx. Insert a 22 gauge (0.71 mm) wire into the base of the stem and push it up into the head. If you find that the flower head spins around, add another wire, using the cross-ply wiring technique on page 132.

Internal wiring

This technique is used in wedding floristry to support soft and hollow-stemmed flowers such as calla lilies. Use 22 gauge (0.71 mm) or 20 gauge (0.90 mm) wire depending on the thickness of the stem and the level of support required.

1 Ease a length of stub wire up the entire stem of the flower, supporting the stem in your hand and manipulating the wire with your thumb. If the wire comes through the stem, stop pushing and withdraw the wire until you can no longer see it. Flex the stem in the other direction and start pushing again carefully. Push the wire up the stem and into the head of the flower.

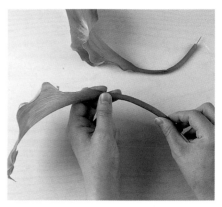

2 Once the wire has been fully inserted into the stem it can be curved to suit the design. Cut off any excess wire unless the soft stem is to be pushed into wet foam, in which case the exposed wire at the base of the stem will act as an extra support.

Wiring delicate flowers

Use this technique for delicate flowers in headdresses, corsages and bouquets. The gauge of the wire will depend on the size and weight of the flower to be wired. With practice, you will be able to judge the weight of the flower and the correct wire gauge to use.

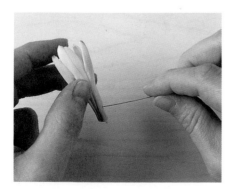

1 Push a 28 gauge (0.38 mm) wire horizontally through the base of the flower head.

2 Bend down the wire and finish off following the method described in step 2 of Loop Stitch on page 130. If additional support is needed, push another wire through the flower base at a right angle to the first wire, pull it down and secure it in the same way.

3 Individual flowers can then be taped together to form a unit following the method described in steps 3 and 4 of Loop Stitch on page 130.

Cross-ply wiring

This technique prevents flower heads twisting and spinning on the original support wire. It can be used for a number of flowers but is particularly useful for roses and orchids. It is used for the bouquet on page 38.

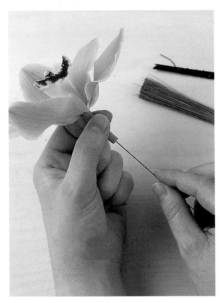

1 Insert a 22 gauge (0.71 mm) wire into the cut stem and push it into the base of the flower head up to where the petals start.

2 Insert a 28 gauge (0.38 mm) silver stub wire through the base of the flower at a right angle to the first wire and fold it down while holding onto the original wire.

3 Secure the two halves of the silver wire to the green wire by wrapping one leg of the silver wire around the other wires.

4 Cover the stem and the wires with florist's corsage tape following the method given in step 3 of Loop Stitch on page 130.

MORE COMPLEX WIRING TECHNIQUES

Wiring and securing stems to a wet foam holder

Flowers can come loose from wet foam holders if they are not secured to the frame. This technique is useful for long-stemmed flowers, especially those used around the edge of the bouquet and large, heavy flowers.

1 Push some of the plant material into the foam and thread a 24 gauge (0.56 mm) wire through the cage.

2 Twist the wire around the stems to anchor them to the cage, then cut off the excess wire.

Wiring for a Carmen rose bouquet

The pure form of the Carmen rose never fails to impress yet is remarkably simple to make. This technique is used to make the Carmen rose bouquet on page 25 in 'Country House'.

1 Place a small wet foam holder in a support, then wire a large, full-petalled rose into the centre of the cage following the method described at left. This will keep the central flower fresh. Set it aside.

3 Holding a group of petals lightly but firmly between the forefinger and thumb of one hand, bend down the ends of the wire and twist them to secure the petals together. Make ten to fifteen groups of petals.

2 Remove the petals from another rose in groups of three or four, taking care not to bruise them. Push lengths of 28 gauge (0.38 mm) silver stub wire through the petals.

4 Push the wire at the base of each group of petals into the wet foam holder prepared in step 1 close to the base of the full, central rose. Bend the petals so that they look like part of the rose. Repeat the process until all the foam is covered and the rose is the desired size. The base of the Carmen rose can be finished with leaves or ribbon.

Making orchid units

This technique is used to create the orchid bouquet on page 38 in 'Putting on the Ritz'.

1 Prepare all the orchids using the cross-ply wiring method on page 132. Cut pieces of 19 gauge (1.0 mm) stay wire to length and tape them with matching florist's corsage tape. Tape the prepared orchids to the stay wires.

2 Tape more, individually wired orchid heads to the stay wires and bind them together to form the long drop of the bouquet, turning each flower so that it can be seen.

OTHER FLORISTRY TECHNIQUES

Using stems as containers

This technique is used to make the centrepiece on page 21 in 'Urban Elegance'.

1 Cut stems of Japanese knotweed or bamboo into short lengths, making sure there is a nodal (sealed) section in each length.

2 Group individual stems together and bind them with string, wire, or tape. (You may want to conceal the tape with raffia or decorative cord.)

3 Stand the groupings on end and fill them with water. Because each section of tube has a watertight nodal membrane, the grouping becomes a natural vase for any flower.

Making free-form wire mesh

This method is used to create the base for the bouquet, corsage and centrepiece on pages 33 and 35 in 'Jewel in the Crown'.

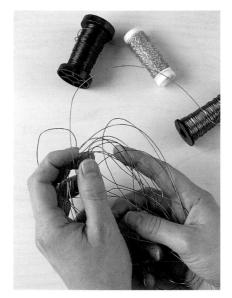

1 Pull off a long length of 24 gauge (0.56 mm) reel wire and press it into a twisted mass. Then fold and shape the wire until you have a tangle of wire of the required length and width.

2 Spray the wire with your chosen colour and let it dry.

3 To create a bouquet, attach the wire to a silk cord in a number of places down its length. The cord will form the main drop of the bouquet and will prevent the wire mesh opening out as plant materials are added.

4 Wire flowers to the cord and the wire mesh to make a free-form arrangement.

Creating pearl stamens

This technique is used to decorate the bouquet on page 100 in 'A Medley of Blooms'.

1 Wire craft or millinery pearls onto pieces of 28 gauge (0.38 mm) silver stub wire and cut to length. Push the wired pearls into the base of a flower so that they burst out as stamens from the centre. The wired flowers can then be taped and used in bouquets, corsages, headdresses or floral displays.

gallery

In this section, you will find all of the main arrangements made in the book. Each piece is accompanied by its page reference and design recipe. Since the arrangements are organised by type, you will be able to compare and contrast different bouquets, headdresses, centrepieces, room decorations and so on, to help you decide which style is right for your wedding.

Refer to the main entries to read about the arrangements in more detail and to see the overall look and feel of the particular wedding. Remember that the arrangements shown may be assembled using flowers of a different type or colour in order to tailor them to your own special day.

FLOWERS TO WEAR OR CARRY
BRIDES' BOUQUETS

Hand-tied bouquet, p.19

5 flamingo flowers
9 Akito roses

Hand-tied bouquet, p.59

10 pieces honeysuckle
10 to 15 grass seed heads
1 honesty stem
10 viburnum stems with berries
5 Vicky Brown roses
2 Peruvian lily stems
4 to 5 St John's wort stems

Hand-tied bouquet, p.65

15 Weber parrot tulips

Hand-tied bouquet, p.81

10 camellia flowers
5 rhododendron flowers
10 pieces cherry blossom
Camellia foliage

Hand-tied bouquet, p.100

15 to 16 lily flower heads
(5 to 7 stems)

Left
Hand-tied bouquet, p.111

10 open ranunculus heads
25 to 30 pieces lily-of-the-valley
9 or 10 pieces brachyglottis
   foliage

Below
Hand-tied bouquet, p.115

3 bouvardia stems
20 to 30 lavender stems
20 sweet pea stems

Cascade

Cascading bouquet, p.35

Wire mesh: ⅔ reel 24 gauge
   (0.56 mm) wire
9 cymbidium orchid heads
5 pieces gloriosa on the vine
3 pieces asparagus fern

Cascading bouquet, p.38

35 individual orchid flowers

Cascading bouquet, p.43

7 calla lilies

Spray

Spray bouquet, p.52

2 orchid stems with 6 or 7
   flowers per stem

Spray bouquet, p.104

5 peonies
7 tuberose stems
1 stephanotis plant
3 mock orange stems

Other

Carmen rose bouquet, p.25

1 main rose
8 to 10 roses for petals

Bride's bag, p.71

2 primrose plants
1 white violet plant
4 spirea stems

Bridal wreath, p.74

12 to 15 pieces lichen
9 or 10 Lenten roses
1 blue hyacinth
1 pink hyacinth
1 plant pink African violets
1 plant purple African violets

Lily stem bouquet, p.90

2 lily stems

BRIDES' HEADDRESSES

Garland headdress, p.115

15 Lord Nelson sweet
   pea buds
1 bouvardia stem
12 sprigs lavender
15 African blue lily pips
6 heads love-in-a-mist

**Carmen rose
hair decoration**, p.24

1 main rose
6 to 8 roses for petals

Hair decoration, p.52

1 vanda orchid flower
2 spikes dogwood
30 hyacinth pips

BRIDESMAIDS' FLOWERS

Crescent headdress, p.57

3 St John's wort stems

Crescent headdress, p.75

½ raceme blue hyacinth
½ raceme pink hyacinth
½ plant blue African violet
½ plant burgundy African violet
1 Lenten rose
8 small pieces lichen

Flower ball, p.27

50 to 60 groups Mexican orange
   blossom flowers
1 stem spray roses

Bridesmaid's bouquet, p.91

1 maidenhair fern plant
10 lily-of-the-valley stems
2 white miniature rose stems

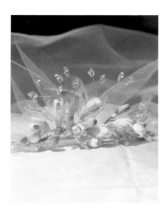

Tiara headdress, p.105

2 tuberose stems
10 wired crystals

Crescent headdress, p.111

6 ranunculus heads
10 pieces lily-of-the-valley

**Bridesmaid's
hand-tied bouquet**, p.106

3 Peruvian lily stems
7 masterwort stems

Floral rope, p.108

2 bunches box foliage
9 ranunculus heads
15 pieces lily-of-the-valley

BRIDESMAIDS' HEADDRESSES

BUTTONHOLES, CORSAGES AND WRISTLET

Garland headdress, p.26

12 to 15 groups Mexican orange
   blossom flowers
12 to 15 rosebuds

Buttonhole, p.20

1 Akito rose
2 scented pelargonium leaves
2 sprigs mahonia berry

Buttonhole, p.27

1 rose
1 piece Mexican orange
   blossom

Shoulder corsage, p.34

Wire mesh: ⅓ reel 24 gauge
   (0.56 mm) wire
7 cymbidium orchids
5 gloriosa heads
1 piece asparagus fern

Crescent headband, p.91

10 lily-of-the-valley stems
6 miniature roses

Buttonhole, p.40

1 moth orchid
3 ivy leaves
2 lilyturf leaves

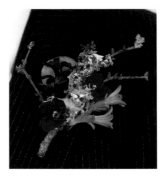

Buttonhole, p.77

5 pink hyacinth flowers
2 blue hyacinth flowers
2 pieces lichen-covered
   larch twig

Corsage, p.76

1 Lenten rose
3 blue hyacinth flowers
3 pink hyacinth flowers
3 pieces lichen

Garland headdress, p.108

25 to 30 pieces lily-of-the-valley

Buttonhole, p.80

1 piece camellia including
   3 leaves
1 lily head
1 piece cherry blossom

Floral wristlet, p.106

1 tuberose stem   5 honesty disks
1 masterwort stem   6 wired crystals

FLOWERS FOR THE TABLE
CENTREPIECES

Centrepiece, p.21

3 proteas
3 flamingo flowers
4 pieces twisted bamboo
2 full stalks Japanese knotweed
  or bamboo cut into pieces
10 Akito roses
3 pieces jasmine
Foliage to fill

Centrepiece, p.28

12 roses
2 maidenhair fern plants
6 to 8 pieces Mexican orange
  blossom
6 pieces Queen Anne's lace

Centrepiece, p.35

9 cymbidium orchids
5 miniature cymbidium orchids
10 atoma gloriosa
3 pieces asparagus fern
13 First Red roses
7 carnation heads

Centrepiece, p.41

3 moth orchid flowers

Centrepiece, p.44

8 calla lilies

Centrepiece, p.48

1 calla lily

Centrepiece, p.51

1 stem vanda orchid

Centrepiece, p.60

10 to 12 Vicky Brown roses
9 to 10 Vienna Blood lily stems
4 protea heads
5 to 6 Peruvian lily stems
8 St John's wort stems
4 Spanish broom stems
Mixed seasonal foliage

Left
Glass tank centrepiece, p.68

40 to 50 tips box foliage
6 to 9 tulip heads

Right
Centrepiece, p.72

3 pink primrose plants
3 yellow primrose plants
8 white violet plants
3 handfuls moss
2 birch branch stems

OTHER TABLE DECORATIONS

Centrepiece, p.85

2 rhododendron racemes
2 magnolia stems
7 pieces pale camellia
5 pieces deep pink camellia
3 pieces Corsican hellebore
Camellia and rhododendron
  foliage to fill

Centrepiece, p.92

The number of stems required
will depend on how many
flowers are open, but 3 stems
should be sufficient for one
centrepiece

Decorated champagne flutes,
p.20

1 Akito rose
1 scented pelargonium leaf
2 sprigs mahonia berry

Floral gift, p.28

1 rose
4 to 5 pieces maidenhair fern
4 to 5 small leaves for the base
2 to 3 pieces Mexican orange
  blossom
A little Queen Anne's lace

Centrepiece, p.113

12 to 15 ranunculus stems with
  buds
10 to 15 pieces lily-of-the-valley
5 pieces Solomon's seal

Centrepiece, p.117

15 to 20 lavender sprigs
1 bellflower stem
1 well-branched eucalyptus stem
10 sweet pea stems
5 love-in-a-mist stems

Place setting, p.49

1 calla lily

Napkin tie, p.61

1 Vicky Brown rose
Small part of a Spanish broom
  stem

Small glass tank, p.67

20 tips box foliage
4 to 6 tulip heads

Napkin ring, p.118

5 lavender sprigs
3 brodiaea heads

CHAIRBACKS

Chairback, p.22

2 flamingo flowers
1 Akito rose
1 piece jasmine

Chairback, p.29

1 maidenhair fern plant
2 roses
2 stems spray roses
2 to 3 pieces Mexican orange
   blossom
3 to 4 pieces Queen Anne's lace

Chairback, p.78

30 pieces lichen

Chairback, p.119

5 lavender sprigs
3 to 5 sweet pea stems
1 brodiaea stem

FLOWERS FOR THE RECEPTION

CAKES

Decorated cake, p.60

15 St John's wort stems

Decorated cake, p.99

Base ring:

15 roses
10 Texas bluebells
10 stocks
2 delphiniums
4 lady's mantle stems

Glass stem base:

2 roses
1 Texas bluebell
3 roses, 1 stock, ½ hydrangea
 head for petals

Cake top arrangement:

½ hydrangea head
6 roses,
3 stocks

Decorated dessert, p.78

Around the meringue:

4 blue hyacinth racemes
3 carnations

*Around the base of the
cake stand:*

10 Lenten roses
1 plant blue African violet
1 plant burgundy African violet
1 pink hyacinth raceme
1 blue hyacinth raceme
20 to 25 pieces lichen

Decorated cake, p.117

Bottom tier:

30 sage flowers

Middle tier:

25 brodiaea flowers

Top tier:

15 African blue lily flowers
10 mixed flowers for the top
 decoration

CONTAINERS

Vase, p.37

10 stems gloriosa on the vine

Side table arrangement, p.39

2 moth orchid stems
1 echeveria
5 Scotch thistle leaves
3 cotoneaster sprigs
2 jasmine stems

Vase, p.50

4 to 5 medium cherry blossom
stems

Wicker cone, p.73

3 yellow primrose plants
1 pink primrose plant
2 white violet plants
1 handful moss

Floral urn, p.84

5 pale rhododendron racemes
3 pieces magnolia
7 pieces camellia
5 stems pale pink lily
5 stems cerise lily
5 long pieces apple blossom
5 calla lilies
3 pieces Corsican hellebore
5 branches Norway maple
Foliage to fill

Floral urn, p.92

20 lily stems
5 maidenhair fern plants

Church window arrangement,
p.103

5 peonies
10 tuberose stems
10 delphinium stems
6 snowball bush stems
6 mock orange stems
5 bellflower stems
4 lilac stems

INDOOR DECORATIONS

Door column, p.47

150 English laurel leaves
30 calla lilies

Tulip tree, p.66

15 willow poles
2 bundles dogwood
2 bunches highbush blueberry
30 parrot tulips
Spanish moss

Staircase decoration, p.71

Each 91 cm (yard):
12 pale pink primrose plants
12 yellow primrose plants
18 bedding-plant-sized white
    violet plants
1 medium bag moss

Mantelpiece display, p.59

6 to 9 Vicky Brown roses
6 to 8 Vienna Blood lily stems
4 protea heads
3 to 4 Peruvian lily stems
5 St John's wort stems
3 Spanish broom stems
Mixed seasonal foliage

Staircase garland, p.83

Each 91 cm (yard):
3 rhododendron racemes
4 pieces magnolia
10 pieces camellia
5 tulips
7 pieces Norway maple
Ivy, camellia and rhododendron
    foliage to fill

OUTDOOR DECORATIONS

Right
Church decoration, p.93

2 lily stems
2 maidenhair fern plants

Welcome wreath, p.102

30 to 40 snowball bush heads
5 peonies

Lavender basket of petals, p.114

1 bunch lavender (approximately 60 stems)
4 roses (or enough petals to fill the basket)
10 lavender sprigs, stripped
30 to 40 sweet pea stems

Left
Church arch, p.96

10 hydrangea heads
40 roses
20 lily stems
20 delphiniums
40 stocks
40 Texas bluebell stems
6 love lies bleeding stems
3 bunches eucalyptus
30 to 40 pieces ivy to fill

Below, **Decorated canopy**, p.97

Each top arrangement:
3 lily stems
5 stocks
1 full stem soapwort
2 love lies bleeding stems
3 Texas bluebell stems

Each base arrangement:
4 lily stems
5 stocks
3 delphiniums
4 Texas bluebell stems

Each pole:
4 pieces ruscus

Curtain decoration, p.116

2 bellflower stems
10 sweet pea stems
2 scabiosa stems
20 lavender stems
2 branched eucalyptus stems

Lantern decoration, p.121

10 lavender stems
10 sweet pea stems
2 eucalyptus stems
5 love-in-a-mist stems

plant directory

This directory includes all of the flowers and foliage used throughout the book. Entries are organised alphabetically by botanical name, with the common name below. A short description is given of each item, together with any special care instructions. For more detailed information on any of the flowers listed, consult your florist or one of the many A–Z plant guides available.

Where relevant, the specific cultivars used in this book have been given. With flowers such as roses, there are so many cultivars that not all of them are available everywhere all of the time. However, you or your florist should be able to make a suitable substitution, matching colour and flower type, from the range available in your area.

Peruvian lilies are originally from the cool mountain area of South America. An abundance of flower heads appears on each stem and they are available in a range of strong colours.

A

Acer platanoides
Norway maple

This medium-to-large tree has delicate lime-green flowers in the spring, winged seed cases later in the summer and golden yellow leaves in the autumn. Young branches are good for large arrangements with a wild feel. Condition cut branches as hard stems.

Adiantum raddianum
Maidenhair fern

The arching fronds of this delicate fern make it well worth using, although it does not like dry atmospheres. Where possible use a whole plant, covering the pot with moss if necessary. Cut fronds should be sprayed with water and placed in the arrangement just before use.

Agapanthus umbelatus 'Intermedia'
African blue lily

Small, trumpet-shaped flowers appear in clusters 15 to 20 cm (6 to 8 in) wide on long, strong stems. Different cultivars show shades of blue from very pale to very deep.It is also available in white.

Alchemilla mollis
Lady's mantle

An excellent garden perennial, lady's mantle is easy to grow and tolerant of most conditions. Fluffy lime-green sprays of flowers appear in early to midsummer and last well when cut.

Alstroemeria aurantiaca
Peruvian lily

This is a good cut flower, available in a wide range of colours, that will last up to 10 days. Buy Peruvian lily stems that have their first flower just opening and condition them as soft stems.

Amaranthus caudatus
Love lies bleeding

These long, tasseled flowers in red or green are beautiful in country style arrangements. It is best to remove the foliage as it shrivels quickly and hides the flowers.

Amaryllis (see *Hippeastrum*)

Anthriscus sylvestris
Queen Anne's lace

The umbels of tiny white flowers on this biennial plant make it perfect for wedding arrangements, especially as a filler for headdresses and bouquets. The flowers last well out of water and do not discolour easily.

Anthurium andreanum 'Avo-Lydia'
Flamingo flower, Tail flower

These coloured flowers are actually modified leaves called spathes, with a protruding, cylindrical creamy white spadix. They will last up to two weeks as cut flowers and prefer warm temperatures. Spraying with water every few days will keep them glossy.

Asparagus densiflorus 'Myersii'
Asparagus fern

Cylindrical, arching plumes of very fine foliage make this an excellent plant to use in floral displays. It does not like a dry atmosphere but responds well to misting with water.

Astrantia major
Masterwort

This hardy perennial is available from most florists. Buy when the majority of flowers are open. The tiny star-shaped flowers are held high above the leaves on long stems and will last 5 or 6 days when cut.

The stem length and flowers of African blue lilies are often sizable enough to be used in large-scale designs. There are also some less common dwarf varieties.

B

Bambusa
Bamboo

The twisted bamboo stems now available are particularly attractive in both shape and colour and may be added to larger arrangements for a modern decorative touch. Large, straight stems may be used to form a base for structured arrangements.

Betula
Birch

These deciduous trees are mainly grown for their ornamental bark and colourful autumn foliage. Birch twigs are slender and slightly flexible, making them useful in arrangements.

Bougainvillea x buttiana
Bougainvillea

The brightly coloured bracts of bougainvillea are adapted leaves, not actual flowers. They are generally not available commercially as cut flowers, but bougainvillea plants are obtainable from garden centres and bracts can be cut from these.

Bouvardia longiflora 'White Charla'

Bouvardia

Long, tubular flowers with four petals are produced as loose terminal clusters. Long, straight stems make bouvardia suitable for large arrangements and hand-tied bouquets. It is also fragrant.

Brachyglottis laxifolia

Brachyglottis

An easy-to-grow foliage plant, the undersides of the leaves have a furry, grey-green covering that gives them a silvery appearance. It lasts well as cut foliage.

Brodiaea laxa (see *Triteleia*)

Buxus sempervirens

Box

Small, oval-shaped evergreen leaves on woody branches are usually seen in gardens as topiary trees or low hedge specimens. Box will last up to three weeks when cut if kept in water in a cool room.

Camellia japonica

Camellia

Glossy green camellia foliage is very robust and lasts well when cut. The very delicate single and double flowers need careful handling or they will bruise. Cut flowers will last about three days in water.

Campanula

Bellflower

Buy bellflowers when the buds are fully developed but not open and condition them in cut-flower food. *C. persicifolia* (peach-leaved bellflower) is about 81 cm (32 in) in height. The stem is straight with blue or white flowers held in loose racemes.

Choisya ternata

Mexican orange blossom

This easily grown evergreen shrub has a lovely spicy fragrance. Small, well-branched pieces are suitable for small- to medium-sized arrangements. Condition before using.

One of the longest lasting of all cut flowers, there are literally hundreds of varieties of chrysanthemums.

Chrysanthemum

Chrysanthemum

Officially this has been reclassified as *Dendranthemum*. These flowers come in a huge range of shapes, sizes and colours. Most varieties will last at least a week in water.

Convallaria majalis

Lily-of-the-valley

Small, bell-shaped flowers hang from apple-green stems 12 to 15 cm (5 to 6 in) in length. One of the most strongly perfumed flowers, lily-of-the-valley is readily available in late spring but can be obtained all year round.

Cornus sericea 'Flaviramea'

Dogwood

Strong, flexible stems can be used as cut foliage in the spring and summer or as bare twigs in the autumn and winter when the bright apple-green shoots are just as attractive. *C. alba* has red stems.

Cotoneaster simonsii

Cotoneaster

Cotoneaster has long, arching sprays of small, oval-shaped leaves in the summer and lovely orange to red berries grouped along the stems in the autumn.

Cymbidium arcadian 'Sunrise Golden Fleece'
Cymbidium orchid

This very popular and widely available orchid lasts well as a cut flower either as a whole stem or as single flower heads.

Cytisus
Broom

All species of broom have an abundance of pealike flowers followed by linear or oblong seedpods. Their long, flexible stems make them a good choice for floristry, as they can be easily manipulated.

D

Delphinium New Century hybrids
Delphinium

This easy-to-grow perennial plant is readily available as a cut flower. Buy when the flowers at the bottom of the flower spike are starting to open. It will last for about four or five days.

Dendranthemum (see *Chrysanthemum*)

Dianthus
Carnation

This excellent cut flower lasts very well both in and out of water. Many new colours have been bred over the past decade, but the cultivars used in this book are the orange 'Raggio de Sole', the pink 'Shocking Pink', the gold 'Harvest Moon' and the pink with purple edge 'Rendez-vous'.

E

Echeveria
Echeveria

A number of varieties of this easy-to-grow succulent plant are available commercially. It can be used in floral displays as a whole plant or cut off at the base of the stem.

Carnations are available in every colour except blue. Many varieties have two- or three-tone petals.

Eucalyptus
Eucalyptus

A number of varieties are available, but all have bluish green glaucous foliage with a slightly spicy scent. Eucalyptus lasts well as a cut foliage and is readily available all year round.

Eustoma
Texas bluebell

Also known as *Lisianthus* and prairie gentian, double and single flowers are available in a wide selection of colours from white to deep purple. Eustoma lasts well as a cut flower.

F

Fallopia japonica
Japanese knotweed

The green-and-red stems of this plant are very attractive and useful for more unusual displays. If it is not available, large bamboo stems may be used in the same way.

Freesia
Freesia

This is a useful flower for wedding floristry as it is found in a range of colours, all with a strong perfume. Buy when the first flower on the stem is open. Freesias will last four or five days.

G

Geranium (see *Pelargonium*)

Gloriosa superba 'Rothschildiana'
Gloriosa

The reflexed petals of this beautiful flower are carmine red with a yellow edge. Remove the stamens as the flower develops, as they can stain fabric.

H

Hedera helix
Ivy

Ivy is a very effective and readily available foliage to use in floral displays that lasts well out of water. Long trails can be used around columns or to hang from garlands. The more mature part of the plant (called bush ivy) is a good filler.

Helleborus argutifolius
Corsican hellebore

Within this large genus of beautiful garden plants, *H. argutifolius* last well as a cut flower. It has groups of small, pale green flowers.

Helleborus orientalis
Lenten rose

Flowers range from white with spots of pink to purple. They last well as cut flowers in water.

Hippeastrum
Amaryllis

The hollow stem of this large flower takes up water quickly. Buy when the flowers are starting to show colour but the buds have not opened. Care in handling is essential as the open flower can bruise easily.

Hyacinthus orientalis
Hyacinth

A large number of cultivars have been raised from *H. orientalis* in a wide colour selection. They can be used on the stem, or single flowers can be threaded onto wires.

Hydrangea macrophylla

Bigleaf hydrangea

Hydrangea flowers must be conditioned well to prevent them from wilting. It is often better to buy plants and cut the flowers from them. If you plan to do this, choose long-stemmed heads from the florist.

Hypericum

St John's wort

This plant is available from Holland all year round and has very pretty berries. A number of cultivars provide some colour variation, from soft pinky cream to dark terracotta and brown.

Jasminum

Jasmine

This is usually found as a climbing pot plant. Two major species are used for wedding floristry, both with similar shaped flowers. *J. polyanthum* has a pink blush to the reverse of the petal and is the most readily available, while *J. officinale* is all white.

The distinct perfume of lavender makes it a very popular flower. It is also highly suitable for drying, as it keeps its colour well.

L

Larix

Larch

Larch trees are coniferous and have attractive foliage with yellow to red autumn colour.

Lathyrus odoratus

Sweet pea

This climbing annual plant is easily grown from seed. A range of delicate colours and beautiful fragrance make it a lovely wedding flower. Old-fashioned varieties such as 'Lord Nelson' and 'Liz Taylor' tend to have the strongest scent.

Lavandula

Lavender

Lavender flowers will last well when cut and they also dry well. Lavender is excellent for sprinkling on floors, releasing a delicate perfume as people walk over it. *L. spica* has elegant, long, grey-blue stems, while *L. spica* 'Munstead' has shorter, deep blue spikes. A blue spiked species with pretty winged petals is French lavender, *L. stoechas*.

Lichen

Lichen, Reindeer moss

Lichen is a wild plant often growing on trees or on the ground in areas with particularly clean air. It is available commercially in small bags and boxes, either natural or dyed in a range of colours. It provides a good base for wreaths.

Lilium

Lily

A wide selection of colours and flower types is available. 'Vienna Blood' is cerise to carmine red while 'Le Rêve' is a pale pink. Pollen sacs should be removed as the flowers open to avoid staining. Lilies open and last well in water.

Longiflorum lilies look stunning in displays and are ideal for tall, floor-standing arrangements.

Lilium longiflorum

Longiflorum lily

Long, trumpet-shaped flowers are borne on elegant stems and last well as a cut flower. Pollen sacs need to be removed as the flowers open as they can stain clothes and the flower petals. Cultivars are mainly white.

Liriope platyphylla

Lily turf

This fibrous-rooted plant makes a good ground cover. The straplike leaves last well out of water and are about 20 to 25 cm (8 to 10 in) in length.

Lonicera periclymenum

Honeysuckle

This beautiful climbing plant has delicate, fragrant flowers throughout the summer months. The trailing tendrils, with or without flowers, give a wild, natural look to any floral arrangement.

Lunaria annua

Honesty

This easy-to-grow plant reaches a height of about 1.37 m (1 1/2 yards) and has small purple flowers. It is mainly prized for the silvery, disklike seed heads that look wonderful when dried.

M

Magnolia x *soulangeana*
Magnolia

Many cultivars of this flowering shrub or small tree species have deep pink to purple flowers. However, this species has large, pinkish-white goblet-shaped flowers that last well if conditioned properly with hot water. The foliage is also useful.

Mahonia japonica
Mahonia

In winter and spring this statuesque shrub has lily-of-the-valley-scented flowers followed by blue-green berries in the early summer. Leaves are evergreen and long-lasting when cut and used in arrangements.

Malus floribunda 'Profusion'
Apple blossom

This small crab apple tree has pale pink and cerise flowers in the spring followed by red crab apples in the late summer and early autumn. It is a lovely tree for the small garden.

Matthiola incana 'Anthony and Cleopatra'
Stock

Stocks are excellent cut flowers with a tremendous amount of scent from each individual spike. Readily available from florists, buy them only if the top buds have not opened. The flowers last about three or four days. Use a flower food containing antibacterial agents if possible and change the water every other day.

N

Nigella damascenia Miss Jekyll series
Love-in-a-mist

These delicate, blue starlike flowers are surrounded by a fine filigree of mid-green foliage. Attractive seedpods are a bonus later in the year.

O

Oncidium 'Golden Showers'
Oncidium orchid

This orchid has delicate sprays of small flowers on fine, arching stems that last about a week in water. It is excellent for all types of wedding designs, from carrying flowers to table arrangements.

Onopordum acanthium
Scottish thistle

The tall flower spikes of this dramatic garden biennial reach up to 1.8 m (6 feet) in height. They are not usually available as a cut flower from florists but are easy to grow from seed. Loose rosettes of foliage in the first year are followed by towering, majestic spikes in the second year.

P

Paeonia lactiflora
Peony

The peony is a wonderful garden plant with large single or double ball-like flowers available in the summer. A good pale pink cultivar is 'Sarah Bernhardt' and a lovely white with a strong perfume is 'Duchesse de Nemours'. Buy flowers when the buds are showing colour. If the buds are tight, they can take a few days to open, so timing is crucial for wedding use.

Peonies are prized by gardeners and commercial growers alike.

Moth orchids need a cool atmosphere and frequent misting to ensure longevity. Handle them with care, as they bruise easily.

Pelargonium graveolens 'Lady Plymouth'
Pelargonium

The beautiful filigree edge to the leaves makes this an attractive foliage for floral arrangements. The leaves are scented and have a light variegation in shades of green and white.

Phalaenopsis amabilis
Moth orchid

Moth orchids have excellent lasting qualities. They can be bought as a plant in flower or as a cut flower with four to eight heads per stem. Availability is year round.

Philadelphus coronarius 'Virginal'
Double mock orange

In early summer, the stems of this large shrub are wreathed in small clusters of double flowers with a delicious mock orange perfume. Cut stems need to be conditioned well in water with shrub plant food added. It is sometimes available to buy as a cut flower, but is more widely available as a shrub to grow.

Polianthes tuberosa
Tuberose

The long flower spikes of tuberose grow up to 91 cm (1 yard) long, but the individual flowers are small and delicate. Flushed with pink at the base, the flowers have a strong scent and may be used individually by snipping them off the spike and wiring them. The stems will last up to two weeks in water.

Ranunculus flowers are available in white, yellow, orange, pink and red and are suitable for drying.

Polygonatum x *hybridium*
Solomon's seal

This species of Solomon's seal is a very graceful garden plant. Its arching stems with pairs of leaves make it useful for cut foliage in arrangements, while the white and green bell-like flowers that hang below the leaves are best seen when the leaves are removed.

Protea cynaroides
King protea

The king protea is the largest and most spectacular of all proteas. It is mostly available as a cut flower from South Africa or Australia and lasts up to ten days. It can also be used as a dried flower.

Prunus avium
Cherry blossom

The erect stems of cherry blossom are wreathed in single flowers and last well in water if conditioned properly. The cultivar used in this book is a small, upright tree.

Prunus laurocerasus
English laurel

This is a very easy-to-grow evergreen shrub, excellent for adding depth and visual weight to an arrangement. It is particularly useful in the winter when other foliages are scarce.

Quercus rubra
Red oak

In the autumn, the foliage of this large tree turns vivid shades of gold to deep red and orange, making it an excellent cut foliage to use. Stems and leaves can be preserved by using the hot-water method.

Ranunculus asiaticus
Ranunculus

Bowl-shaped ranunculus flowers resemble small peonies. They are available in bright or pastel shades in late winter and early spring. Double and single flowers are available and will last up to about a week in water.

Rhododendron
Rhododendron

Many rhododendrons are available in a huge range of colours and flower shapes. If you wish to use rhododendrons in quantity, the common lilac-shaded species *R. ponticum* is readily available.

Rosa hybrida
Florist's rose

There is a vast selection of roses from which to choose, many with subtle shades and perfumes. Roses are available all year round which will allow a bride to base her colour scheme on them without any problem at all. The cultivars used in this book are 'Akito', 'Osiana', 'First Red', 'Vicky Brown' and 'Candy Bianca', though other cultivars with similar colours may easily be substituted for them. White miniature roses are also used.

Rosmarinus officinalis
Rosemary

This strongly aromatic evergreen shrub has erect stems wreathed in needlelike foliage. Easy to grow from cuttings, rosemary can be sprinkled on the floor for people to walk over, creating a wonderful perfume as it is crushed.

Ruscus aculeatus
Butcher's broom

This species of ruscus has small, pointed, dark green leaves on long, arching stems. Its small leaves make it excellent for garlands.

Saintpaulia hybrida Rhapsodie strain
African violet

This excellent houseplant comes in a range of colours and flowers are plain, filled or double. It is easy to use in displays as a whole plant by wrapping the pot in moss. The flowers also last very well out of water.

Salix
Willow

Willow branches are good for creating large structures, as they are not brittle. Twisted willow stems (*S. contorta*) may be used decoratively in larger arrangements.

Salvia officinalis
Culinary sage

This is a useful garden plant, as it is both decorative and useful in cooking. The leaves can be used in arrangements; however, in this book, the blue flowers have been used.

Saponaria officinalis
Soapwort

Small, star-shaped pink or white flowers are carried on stems about 20 cm (8 in) long. Handle with care as the stems break easily.

Scabiosa caucasica 'Clive Greaves'
Scabiosa

Flat flowers 5 to 8 cm (2 to 3 in) in diameter are carried on straight, elegant stems 50 to 70 cm (20 to 28 in) in length. It needs to be bought as the flowers are starting to open.

Sorbus aucuparia

Rowan

A small, deciduous tree with delicate, fernlike leaves, rowan is usually used in the autumn for its scarlet berries.

Sphagnum

Sphagnum moss, Moss

This readily available moss is excellent for disguising plant pots or florist's foam at the base of floral arrangements.

Spartium junceum

Spanish broom

This easy-to-grow garden shrub has bright yellow flowers on long, quill-like stems. In this book, stems wreathed with seedpods have been used.

Spiraea 'Arguta'

Spirea

Spirea is a hardy deciduous shrub with white sprays of flowers on long stems. Cut when the flowers are starting to open and condition well as spirea tends to wilt easily.

Stephanotis floribunda

Stephanotis

This climbing houseplant likes temperatures above 15°C (60°F). Clusters of flowers on the vine-like stems have a very delicate perfume.

Syringa vulgaris 'Madame Lemoine'

Double white lilac

A small garden tree with panicles of double white flowers, this lilac flowers earlier in the year than most varieties.

Tulips are native to Turkey, Iran, Syria and parts of Asia. Their name originates from the Turkish word tiilbend, meaning turban.

Tillandsia usneoides

Spanish moss

This moss is actually a type of air plant and has fine, mosslike foliage in pale, dusty grey.

Triteleia laxa 'Koningin Fabiola'
(syn. *Brodiaea laxa*)

Brodiaea

Loose terminal clusters of small, trumpet-shaped flowers are found on elegant stems 20–28 in. (50–71 cm) in length. Buy when a few flowers in the cluster have opened. It will last up to two weeks as a cut flower.

Brodiaea is a small lily originally from California. 'Koningin Fabiola' is the most common variety.

Tulipa

Tulip

Tulips come in a massive range of colours, shapes and types, from species to named cultivars. In this book, the parrot tulip 'Weber' was used along with the soft pink 'Christmas Dream'. They are handy for creating a packed style of arrangement, but note that they will still grow for up to 24 hours after cutting.

Vaccinium corymbosum

Highbush blueberry

The fine stems can be used without leaves to make a delicate framework in which other flowers can be placed, or they can be clipped tight to form a hedge effect. Stems last well out of water in the winter.

Viburnum opulus

Snowball bush

Sometimes known as guelder rose, this viburnum is grown for the round panicles of tiny flowers that look like snowballs. The flowers start life green and turn creamy white as they age.

Viburnum tinus

Viburnum

An evergreen shrub, this viburnum is grown for its small, delicate, pale pink-flushed flowers in the early spring and for its blue berries in the late summer and early autumn.

Zantedeschia

Calla lily

There are a whole range of these flowers now available. *Z. aetheopica* is the white-spathed lily sometimes called Easter lily and the cultivar 'Green Goddess' has a green tip to the end of the spathe. *Z. Rehmannii* has a smaller spathe and has been bred into a wide range of colours, while a bright yellow, large-spathed species is *Z. elliottiana*.

index

ACKNOWLEDGMENTS

The author and the publishers would like to thank the following people and organisations for their help in making this book possible:

Mona Vora (www.monavora.com) for providing the wedding dress on page 33; Johanna Hehir (www.johannahehir.com) for providing the wedding dresses on pages 52 and 71; Gaynor Williams and Stephanie Maltby at The Bridal House, Chester (www.bridal-house.co.uk) for providing all other dresses.

Jill Broadfoot for the cakes.

Viscount and Viscountess Ashbrook, Jenny and Jeffery Lee and Robert Patrick Newman for allowing us to photograph in their homes.

Mr and Mrs John Gallon and Mrs. Judy Poley at Arley Hall (www.arleyestate.zuunet.co.uk).

Robin Llywelyn, Meic Williams, Russell Sharp and all the staff at Port Meirion and Castell Deudreath (www.portmeirion-village.com).

Alison, Fabien and Uma Bernard; Nia Deakin; Katy Denny; Benjamin Ellis Doughty; Nia and Elin Evans; Jenny Lee; Robert Patrick Newman; Siona Alaw Pritchard; Janet Ravenscroft and her dog Houdi; and Ceri Roberts for acting as models.

Special thanks go to Sheila McGibbon and Neil Hamman for their tremendous help in creating the floral arrangements and to Ffion Roberts for her invaluable assistance.

Photographed by Shona Wood
Designed by Janet James
Index prepared by Richard Bird
Edited by Katy Denny and Helen Huckle
Project managed by Janet Ravenscroft

More of Stephen Roberts' floral designs can be seen on www.countrygardenflorist.co.uk.